THE ROLE OF THE STATE IN PENSION PROVISION: EMPLOYER, REGULATOR, PROVIDER

THE ROLE OF THE STATE IN PENSION PROVISION: EMPLOYER, REGULATOR, PROVIDER

Edited by

Gerard Hughes

The Economic and Social Research Institute, Dublin

and

Jim Stewart

Trinity College, Dublin

KLUWER ACADEMIC PUBLISHERS

BOSTON / DORDRECHT / LONDON

A C.I.P. Catalogue record for this book is available from the Library of Congress.

ISBN 0-7923-8433-4

Published by Kluwer Academic Publishers,
P.O. Box 17, 3300 AA Dordrecht, The Netherlands.

Sold and distributed in North, Central and South America
by Kluwer Academic Publishers,
101 Philip Drive, Norwell, MA 02061, U.S.A.

In all other countries, sold and distributed
by Kluwer Academic Publishers,
P.O. Box 322, 3300 AH Dordrecht, The Netherlands.

Printed on acid-free paper

IN MEMORIAM

Toini Christiansson

1947-1997

CONTENTS

YUNG-PING CHEN is an economist who holds the Frank J. Manning Eminent Scholar's Chair, Gerontology Institute, University of Massachusetts Boston. A founding member of the National Academy of Social Insurance, he served on the Panel of Actuaries and Economists of the 1979 Advisory Council on Social Security.

TOINI CHRISTIANSSON (deceased) was Head of the Department of Social Policy at Abo Akademi in Finland where she also worked as a research manager. She was the author of many publications on pension security in Finland.

PETER CONNELL works in Information Systems Services in Trinity College. He has developed a demographic projection model which has been used by the Central Statistics Office, the National Council for the Elderly, and the ESRI to make long range population projections for Ireland.

BRYN DAVIES is an actuary based in London. He provides advice to trade unions on supplementary pension plans. He also writes on pensions and is the author of reports for the Institute of Public Policy Research in the U.K. on reforming occupational pensions and is co-author with Sue Ward of a report on women and personal pensions for the equal Opportunities Commission.

TERESA GHILARDUCCI is an associate professor of economics at the University of Notre Dame in South Bend, Indiana. She received her doctorate in economics from the University of California at Berkeley. She is the author of *Labor's Capital: The Economics and Politics of Private Pensions (1992)*.

GERARD HUGHES is an economist at The Economic and Social Research Institute in Dublin. He is the author of reports on social security and civil service pensions in Ireland. He has acted as a consultant to the OECD on pensions and labour market issues and is the author of the OECD country report on private pensions in Ireland.

DAGMA KNIEP-TAHA is a pensions expert in the Federal Ministry of the Interior in Bonn.

ERIK LUTJENS is a pension lawyer and partner with the law firm of Derks-Star Busmann in Amsterdam in the Netherlands. He is also a professor in pension law at the Free University of Amsterdam and has written extensively on legal and other aspects of pensions.

TONY LYNES has worked in the field of social security and pensions for nearly 40 years. After qualifying as a Chartered Accountant, he worked with Professor

Richard Titmuss at the London School of Economics from 1958 to 1965, became the first full-time secretary of the Child Poverty Action Group in 1966, and was a social security adviser to Labour Party Secretaries of State from 1974 to 1979. Under the Conservative Governments of 1979-1997 he assisted Labour Party shadow social security ministers. His past publications include books and pamphlets on pensions, the *Penguin Guide to Supplementary Benefits* and a weekly column on benefits in *New Society* and the *New Statesman*.

FINN OSTRUP is an associate professor at the Copenhagen Business School's Institute of Finance. He has worked for the Ministry of Economics in Denmark and has served on government committees on national pensions policy and contributed to government reports on pensions.. He has written a number of books and articles on the Danish financial system and is a member of the European Commission's Network of Experts on Supplementary Pensions.

EINAR OVERBYE is Research Director of the social security unit at NOVA - Norwegian Social Research, a government sponsored research institute in Oslo. He received his doctorate in political science from the University of Oslo. He has studied social security issues since 1987, with a special emphasis on the public-private mix. He has written extensively on occupational pensions, including public service pensions with particular reference to the Scandinavian countries and he has also written on pension politics in Australia, New Zealand, and the United States.

DAVID RAJNES is completing his doctorate at Johns Hopkins University. His dissertation examines financial aspects of privatising pension systems in Hungary and other transition economies. The author of several articles on international pension issues, he is employed by the US Bureau of the Census, where he works on a number of major surveys dealing with labour and welfare issues.

JIM STEWART is a lecturer in finance in the School of Business Studies at Trinity College. He is interested in pension funds as shareholders and their influence on corporate governance. He has undertaken research on the effects of pension funds on capital markets.

JOHN TURNER is a senior economist at the International Labour Office in Geneva. He has been doing research on policy issues concerning social security and occupational pensions for over two decades for the US social security department and the US Department of Labor. He has a PhD in economics from the University of Chicago. He is an adjunct lecturer at George Washington University, where he teaches the economics of ageing. He is the author or editor of numerous articles and books on social security and occupational pensions including "Securing Employer Based Pensions" which was published last year by the Pension Research Council in the United States.

SUE WARD is an independent pensions consultant. She has worked for the Trades Union Congress and is the author of *The Essential Guide to Pensions* (Pluto Press, 1990), *The Pensions Handbook* (Age Concern Books, 1998), *Women and Personal Pensions* (HMSO, 1992) (with Bryn Davies) and a number of other books and articles on the subject. She is also a member of the Board of the Occupational Pensions Authority.

Acknowledgements

The chapters in this book are based on papers presented at the European Network for Research on Supplementary Pensions conference "Public Service Pensions Policy Issues" and seminar on "Rebalancing Supplementary and State Pensions in the E.U and the U.S." which were organised by the editors and held in Trinity College Dublin, Ireland on 27-28 September 1997. The meetings were made possible by support from Ireland's *Commission on Public Service Pensions,* the Economic and Social Research Institute, Dublin, Trinity College, Dublin, and the Observatoire des Retraites, Paris.

We gratefully acknowledge the support which The Economic and Social Research Institute has given us in preparing the book for publication. We are grateful to Regina Moore for the care and efficiency with which she converted the papers to a uniform camera-ready layout and to Pat Hopkins for solving the problem we had with the charts in Chapter 12.

Gerry Hughes & Jim Stewart
The Economic and Social Research Institute, Dublin
Trinity College, Dublin

Part I THE STATE AS EMPLOYER

1 INTRODUCTION: INCREASING PENSION COSTS AND THE COMPLEXITY OF THE STATE'S ROLE

Gerard Hughes and Jim Stewart

Introduction

Concerns have emerged about the increasing cost of pension schemes in a number of OECD countries in recent years. Such concerns are not new. In a comment on a book on Social Security in China Chen (1995) points out that a Government report on pensions for high Government officials concluded that:

> "Because of the rising volume of retirement cases over the years, it is our recommendation that a one-third reduction in pension benefits be instituted at the earliest opportune time...".

This was written more than 2,000 years ago during the Han dynasty (206 B.C.-220 A.D). Today the State's involvement as an employer in the pension system generally includes central and local Government and non-commercial public corporations. For employees of these organisations the State cannot just focus on issues relating to pension conditions, affordability, and comparability with the private sector. To its initial role as an employer it has added roles as a provider of social insurance pensions for the labour force and as a regulator of occupational and private pension schemes. These different roles place constraints on the State's capacity for unilateral action. Recall the events in France and Italy some years ago where attempts by the Government to cut public service and social insurance pension benefits brought economic life to a standstill until negotiations took place with the other pension system actors (private sector employers, trade unions, and pensioners representatives).

The State's roles as provider and regulator have led protagonists in the debate on privatisation of pensions to focus attention on the mechanisms used to finance pensions for public sector employees: should pension schemes for the State's own employees continue to be financed on a pay-as you-go basis or through the accumulation of employer and employee contributions in a pension fund? Funded pensions invariably rely on private service providers such as stock brokers, auditors, investment specialists, actuaries, and lawyers. Hence, the State has to consider whether it should hive off its financial responsibility for its own employees pensions to private sector organisations which can provide these services or administer the fund itself. In addition, the State must also consider social insurance pensions because they affect the final pension which public sector employees will receive. Total income received from social insurance pensions and occupational pensions is an important aspect of the design of pension systems since it is possible that post retirement income could be higher than income at work. Due to the cost, and possible incentive effects, replacement rates of post retirement incomes are often targeted at two-thirds of pre-retirement incomes. Even in the case of low income employees there is a general reluctance by employers to establish post retirement income at more than 100% of pre-retirement income. Thus, State pension provision to its own employees involves consideration of funding, regulation and integration with social insurance pensions. The papers in this book show how the State in different countries in the OECD has dealt with these issues as an employer and how its roles as pension regulator and provider are changing.

The State as Employer

In Part I an overview is provided for some OECD countries of how the State's role as employer, regulator, and provider is now being exercised. In Chapter 2 Bryn Davies provides a summary of public service pension arrangements in Denmark, France, Germany, the Netherlands, the United Kingdom, and the United States. Einar Overbye presents in Chapter 3 a detailed analysis of the politics of public service pensions and how they interact with broader social and political issues, based on experience in Norway. The broad issues identified in Bryn Davies paper are taken up in Chapter 4 by Erik Lutjens paying particular attention to the recent privatisation of public service pensions in the Netherlands. Finn Ostrup considers how public service pensions are funded in Denmark in Chapter 5 and Dagmar Kniep-Taha reports on the debate on funding public service pensions in Germany in Chapter 6. In Chapter 7 John Turner and David Rajnes look at the reform of the pension system for Federal Government employees in the United States and show how the new Federal Employee Retirement System is less generous for career civil servants than the old Civil Service Retirement System.

Part I considers a number of issues relating to pensions for public sector employees. A key question is: how much are public service pensions likely to cost in the future? For some countries it is difficult to answer this question because public sector pension schemes are, generally, not run on actuarial lines. However, long-range estimates do exist for Germany, the Netherlands, and the United States. They show that costs are likely to increase significantly in the future, although the percentage of national resources which will have to be allocated to public service pensions will not necessarily increase to the same extent because the economy itself will be growing over the relevant period.

Almost all developed countries established occupational pension schemes for some categories of public servants before the State social insurance pension scheme. So another question which arises is: do public servants contribute towards the cost of their pension scheme? Public servants can contribute either explicitly by direct contribution or implicitly by a reduction in salary. In Norway and Germany public service employee contributions are implicit via a reduction in salary while in the United States the employee contribution is explicit. Although hard evidence is not available for the other countries Bryn Davies paper suggests there is little difference between the pension contributions paid, explicitly or implicitly, by public and private sector employees provided that the contributions to social insurance and occupational pension schemes are both taken into account. This conclusion is also true for Ireland. (see Hughes (1988))

Most developed countries finance public service pensions on a pay-as-you-go basis. Concern over the emerging costs of these schemes has led to renewed interest in funding as a possible means of reducing the burden on the taxpayer. The main arguments in favour of funding public service pensions seem to be based on considerations which are appropriate to private rather than public sector organisations. The paper by Dagmar Kniep-Taha argues that attempts to fund public service pension schemes by two Länder in Germany resulted in increased costs and had to be abandoned. This echoes the finding of a joint committee of the Civil Service National Whitley Council in the United Kingdom. This committee concluded that there would be no great advantage in funding civil service pensions because where the central Government is the employer the security of the benefits is guaranteed by the Government, and no greater security would be achieved by setting up a fund (see Nottage (1975)).

The State as Pension Regulator

Part II deals with issues of pension regulation. The greater the reliance on private sector pension provision the greater the role of State regulation. Chapter 8 is written by Sue Ward who was a member of the Goode Committee established to enquire into pension provision in the U.K. following the Maxwell scandal. She is currently a member of the U.K. Occupational Pensions Regulatory Authority (OPRA). Her chapter provides a detailed account of current issues relating to pensions regulation. Of particular interest is the evolution of pension regulation from tax compliance to monitoring and standard setting for financial products providing pensions. In Chapter 9 Tony Lynes considers the background to pension reform in the U.K. undertaken by the previous Conservative Government and the present Labour Government. He argues that proposals to provide second pensions through private money-purchase stakeholder pension schemes have major disadvantages and he outlines the advantages which the State Earnings-Related Pension Scheme has over other second pension schemes. Chapter 10 by Erik Lutjens summarises the complex debate relating to reform of the Dutch pension system. Debate about reform in the Netherlands takes place in the context of projections of rising costs, the role of the State in pension provision, and whether membership of occupational schemes should be mandatory.

The State as Pension Provider

In the countries whose experience is considered in this book the State plays an important role as a provider of public pensions. It is possible for State employees in these countries to receive both an occupational pension and a social insurance pension. Proposals for reform are largely driven by cost considerations due to demographic change. Cost considerations and the need to adapt pension policy to workforce patterns have also led to proposals to 'privatise pensions'. These issues are considered in Part III. The paper by Peter Connell and Jim Stewart critically examines forecasts of demographic change for Ireland. Forecasts of demographic change are shown to be quite sensitive to assumptions about in-migration. They argue that population ageing need not necessarily result in rising pension costs since its effect may be offset by other factors such as rising labour force participation rates. Chapter 13 by the late Toini Christiansson deals with the effects of indexation reforms in Finland on the overall costs of pensions as a per cent of GDP and the effects of these reforms on replacement rates. She concludes from an analysis of data provided by the Finnish Ministry of Health and Social Affairs that the indexation reforms have widened the disparity between the incomes of those who are at work and those who are retired. Economists have developed a number of models, reflecting different theoretical perspectives, to explain how society determines the distribution of income between the working and the retired population. In Chapter 12 Teresa Ghilarducci derives testable hypotheses about pensions expenditure from models of intergenerational, class, sectoral, and gender conflict. In the final chapter, Bing Chen considers the debate over the cost of social security in the United States. He argues that the solution to mounting costs is not to dismantle defined benefit social security pensions but to combine them with an individual savings/investment account which could be used to provide an individual pension supplement of the defined contribution type.

References

Chen, Yung-Ping, "Providing Economic Security for the Older Population: Public or Private Approaches". Remarks for Plenary Session on Social and Behavioural Sciences, 5th Asia/Oceania Congress of Gerontology, Hong Kong, 21 November, 1995.

Hughes, G. *The Irish Civil Service Superannuation Scheme*. Dublin: The Economic and Social Research Institute, 1988.

Nottage, R. *Financing Public Sector Pensions*. London: Royal Institute of Public Administration, 1975.

2 PUBLIC SERVICE PENSION ARRANGEMENTS IN DEVELOPED COUNTRIES

Bryn Davies

Introduction

This paper provides a brief outline of the different systems used for pension provision for public service employees in developed countries. It makes clear that there is no single form of pension provision for such employees, with variation both between countries and between different groups of public service employees within countries.

A major problem encountered in making comparisons of pension provision is the scope for ambiguity and confusion that arises in relation to the technical terms that have to be used. Here there is additional scope for confusion over what we mean by the terms "public service" and "developed countries".

As far as technical pension terms are concerned there is scope for confusion about what particular terms mean while theoretical distinctions are not always as precise in practice as they might be in theory. For example, the term "funded schemes" usually means schemes that pay benefits principally from accumulated assets built up over the member's period of active employment, but the term is sometimes employed for book provision arrangements where assets are held only notionally. Such issues of terminology should be as unambiguous as possible and Appendix I provides a short glossary of how some key terms are used in this paper.

The further problem is that there is no simple definition of what is meant by "the public service". Despite the widespread trend to reduce the scope of the public sector, there are still many developed countries with substantial workforces employed in different ways by the State. It is assumed that we are not only looking at employees of the central organs of the State, i.e. employees often described by the term "civil servants", but also at public service workers more widely. This creates the problem that groups that might be in the public service in some countries are in the private sector in others, e.g. health workers. However, at the risk of some oversimplification, the employees concerned can be usefully considered in the following sectors:

- central government employees, i.e. employees of the central or federal government;

7

- local government employees, i.e. employees of subsidiary tiers of elected government including states, regions, municipalities, public education and health authorities;
- employees of public corporations, run on noncommercial lines.

Including the employees of those commercial organisations that are publicly owned would also be possible, but for the purposes of the present discussion it is assumed that these are excluded. In any event, such organisations generally appear to have similar provision to that of comparable privately owned companies.
The paper also requires a view on what is meant by the term "developed countries". While this is an issue that raises a number of points of principle, for the purpose of simplicity it is taken to mean countries that are members of the OECD.

Given this background the paper looks in turn at:

- the issues that determine the structure of pension provision for public service employees in different countries, within the context of that countries pension provision more generally;
- some illustrations of the ways in which public service pensions are provided in particular developed countries; and
- general conclusions about how public service pensions are provided, based on these international comparisons.

Pensions in the Public Sector

The main focus of this paper is on the provision made specifically for public service workers in each country. However, such provision is made within the general structure of pension provision established for the country concerned and a description of the former only makes sense when set against a description of the latter.

Considering pension provision as a whole, all developed countries now have well-established pension structures covering all employees, both in the public and the private sector. In all cases there is a mandatory State pension system which is intended to ensure universal coverage. In addition most of these countries also have significant supplementary (sometimes termed "complementary") arrangements to provide all or some workers with benefits in addition to the basic benefits provided by the State. Such additional benefits are mandatory for all employees in some countries but in others they are voluntary, either at the option of the employer or the employee.

It is not possible to provide a detailed description of every type of national system of pension provision in the present paper, although this information is available from other sources. It is important, however, to understand that there are important differences between virtually all the countries concerned. Nevertheless, it is possible to identify the following main types of structure, within which public service pension arrangements have to operate:

- a predominate State scheme, providing a level of earnings-related benefits that is adequate on its own, with supplementary arrangements having a limited role, e.g. Germany;
- a substantial State scheme, providing a minimum level of earnings-related benefits, plus supplementary arrangements that have an important role in providing an adequate overall income for all or some employees, e.g. France and USA; and
- a limited State scheme, providing a flat-rate benefit, possibly means-tested, with supplementary arrangements required to provide an adequate retirement income, other than for employees on the lowest levels of pay while at work, e.g. Denmark, Netherlands and United Kingdom.

Given a country's general structure of pension provision the specific provision that is made for public service employees can be put into context. One possibility is that public service pension arrangements will be identical to those for employees more generally. In practice, however, this appears to be rarely the case. What does appear to be the case, however, is that the particular arrangements adopted for public service provision in each country are hardly ever the result of a comprehensive plan based on first principles. Usually they appear to be simply the result of history, depending for example on whether particular arrangements for public service employees originated before or after a State scheme was established for the workforce as a whole.

Given the scope for variation in the structure of national pension provision and then the range of possible arrangements specifically for the public service, there is a large number of potential outcomes. However, given the general structure for a particular country, the key parameters that describe public service provision are:

- its relationship to the general structure of pension provision, and in particular, whether it replaces the main State pension or is in addition to it and, in the latter case, whether and how benefits are adjusted to allow for State benefits;
- the institutional structure of public service pension provision and how it is funded; and
- the sort of benefits that are provided and, in particular, whether the guarantee that is given is established in terms of defined benefits or defined contributions.

The above list of issues is not intended to be exhaustive. Some other important issues also arise in relation to public service schemes, such as the arrangements made for transfers between schemes within and outside the public sector; whether there are arrangements for contracting-out of part of the State scheme (what the Americans call "pay or play"); the extent to which benefits are index-linked and how this compares with such protection in the private sector; the tax treatment of contributions and benefits and how this compares with such provisions in the private sector; and whether membership of public service schemes is compulsory or voluntary. However, to ensure the paper is of a manageable length and to keep the focus on the most important issues, these additional points are not covered in the present paper in any detail.

There is also the question of what levels of pension are produced by public service schemes. This would be relevant both in comparison with private sector employees in the same country and in making comparisons of provision between countries. Despite its importance this issue is not dealt with in this paper. This is partly because there is little of the information required to make such comparisons readily available and, even if the information were available, such comparisons are notoriously difficult to make.

Examples of Public Service Provision

This section provides a brief description of how pensions are provided for public service employees in a range of specific countries. The choice of countries is not intended to provide a statistically sound sample of all developed countries but has been determined simply to provide some useful examples of the range of different approaches that have been adopted in practice. More detailed descriptions for some countries are provided in later chapters.

Denmark: The general system of pension provision is a universal State basic flat-rate pension plus a system of supplementary funds. The supplementary funds are negotiated and effectively compulsory, with most of them now established as "labour market pension schemes", i.e. on a branch or industry-wide basis, with defined contributions. There is also a limited and declining number of older established single employer schemes that offer defined benefits.

Public service employees all participate in the basic State system. In addition a proportion, mainly within public administration and the school system, belong to defined benefit schemes financed on a pay-as-you-go basis. The remainder belong to a number of the labour market funds, each covering a broad area of employment.

France: The general system of pension provision is a near universal State basic pension, the Social Security General Scheme, plus a system of supplementary funds covering all employees. These are all established on a pay-as-you-go basis, with the supplementary schemes operating on a "repartition" system.

Most public service employees, including those in public corporations, belong to one of a number of what are described as Social Security Special Schemes. These replace both the Social Security General Scheme and the supplementary scheme that would be offered in the private sector, for the employees concerned. The only significant group of public employees not in a Special Scheme is those on short-term contracts who receive benefits from the General Scheme plus their own supplementary scheme.

Germany: The general system of pension provision is a near universal State scheme that provides defined benefits through a system of autonomous pay-as-you-go schemes. In addition over half the employed workforce belong to one of a number of supplementary schemes that provide relatively limited defined benefits and are usually, but not universally, established on a book provision basis.

Most public service employees belong to the State scheme and are also members of one of a number of pay-as-you-go supplementary schemes, that provide limited additional benefits that are integrated with the State system. There is a group of federal employees, however, i.e. those with the formal status of permanent civil servants, who have their own scheme and do not belong to the normal State scheme. This scheme is funded from general taxation, without any reserves being built up, and provides benefits that are broadly equivalent to those of other public service employees, although precise comparisons are difficult because of differences in their tax treatment.

Netherlands: The general system of pension provision is a universal State basic flat-rate pension plus a well developed system of supplementary funds. The supplementary funds are negotiated and are effectively compulsory, offering defined benefits on a funded basis. Many are established on a single employer basis with a growing number on a branch or industry-wide basis, but all of them offer defined benefits.

Public service employees all participate in the basic State system. They also all belong to a limited number of large supplementary schemes, with funded benefits. The fund for Civil Servants, the ABP, is reported to be the largest pension fund in Europe.

United Kingdom: The general system of pension provision is a universal State basic flat-rate pension plus the State Earnings Related Pension Scheme (SERPS). In addition, nearly half of all employees belong to a supplementary scheme, which is typically established on a funded, defined benefit basis. Where the supplementary scheme meets a defined standard the employer can decide that its employees should be contracted-out of SERPS, in return for paying lower social security contributions.

The great majority of public service workers belong to supplementary schemes that are contracted-out, i.e. they do not accrue entitlement to SERPS benefits. The schemes for employees of central government, e.g. civil servants, police, armed forces, provide defined benefits and are mostly established on a pay-as-you-go basis, although the teachers' scheme is notionally funded. Employees of local government and public corporations belong to funded schemes with defined benefits.

United States of America: The general system of pension provision is a State scheme, known as Social Security, that provides defined benefits on a notionally funded basis. In addition, about half the employed workforce belongs to some sort of supplementary arrangement, although these vary widely in their structure. There is still a large number of funded defined benefit schemes but there is a growing proportion of members in individual funded arrangements providing benefits on a defined contribution basis.

Public service employees are almost universally covered by arrangements that are sponsored by their own employer, although these are run on a collective basis within a number of individual states. These arrangements are mostly on a defined benefit basis but there are now also a number of defined contribution schemes. In many cases, but not all, the employees concerned do not belong to the Social Security system, the decision on this being up to the employer concerned. Schemes for federal employees are financed on a pay-as-you-go basis but otherwise schemes in the public sector are funded, producing some of the largest investment institutions in the world.

Conclusions

This section of the paper sets out some general observations about the ways in which pensions are provided for public service employees, based on a comparison of such provision in developed countries. The key issues that have been considered in making the comparison of public service provision are:

- the structure of public service pension provision;
- its relationship to the general structure of pension provision; and the sort of benefits that are provided.

The most obvious conclusion is that there is no single pattern of provision for the public service, with significant differences in how provision is made, not only between countries but also between different sections of the public service within them.

However, it is still possible to identify some general points and these are set out below. It needs to be stressed that none of these are absolute rules and in each case it would be possible to point to one or more exceptions.

In nearly all developed countries there are special arrangements for at least some public service employees, i.e. they differ from the norm for employees in the private sector. In most cases, however, these appear to be the results of history, rather than as a specific response to the specific requirements of the public service employees concerned.

Employees of lower tiers of government and public corporations typically have separate arrangements that are financed in the same way that pensions are financed in the private sector.

In almost all developed countries the employees of the central organs of the State, i.e., those employees often described as "civil" servants, have arrangements financed on a pay-as-you-go basis. The only exception is the Netherlands where the switch to a funded basis occurred relatively recently.

Most countries provide pensions for their public service employees through defined benefit schemes but there are some exceptions, for at least part of the public sector workforce, e.g. in Denmark and the USA.

It does not appear to be the case that public service employees are especially favoured in the level of their pension benefits, when compared to private sector employees in comparable employments. The main differences in levels of benefit, as between public and private sectors, arise in those countries where supplementary schemes are voluntary and, as a result, significant sections of the private sector labour force have no supplementary provision.

Appendix I

Glossary of Main Pension Terms used in the Paper

Assets: The investments actually held by a pension scheme to meet current or future liabilities, held in the form of one of more of the following securities: cash and deposits; government securities; corporate bonds; equity or ordinary shares; property; and their derivatives.

Basic pension: The minimum level of pension benefit provided by the State for the generality of employees or citizens, usually but not always on a flat-rate basis,

Book provision: A type a pension arrangement where the benefits are paid from a notional book provision established by the employer over the member's period of active service.

Complementary Pension: Means essentially the same as "supplementary pension" (qv).

Defined benefits: Benefits which are based on the individual member's own service and earnings record. The earnings taken into account can be averaged over the member's working lifetime or over a shorter period near to or at retirement.

Funded: A type of pension arrangement where the benefits are paid principally from real assets that have been built up over a member's period of active employment. The assets are accumulated from contributions paid by the employee and/or the employer.

Pay-as-you-go: Pension arrangement where benefits are paid out of contributions currently being paid by and on behalf of active members where assets are only held for the purposes of short-term liquidity. The payments might be made by an autonomous body, funded by the members and/or the employer, or paid directly by the employer out of its own finances.

Pension: A regular payment to a retired employee, normally paid from their retirement until their death.

Pension Scheme: An autonomous body for collecting contributions, paying pensions and, if appropriate, investing the assets held in the fund.

Supplementary Pension: A pension that supplements or complements a basic pension (qv). There are a number of different ways in which supplementary or complementary pensions are provided, but typically they are either sponsored by individual employers or organised on an industry-wide (or branch-wide) basis.

3 THE POLITICS OF PUBLIC SERVICE PENSIONS

Einar Overbye

Introduction

The state performs three pension-political roles. First, it provides public pensions. Second, it regulates the private – including the occupational – pension sector. Third, it provides occupational pensions for its own employees. The three roles as provider, regulator and employer are in principle separate from each other, but in practice tend to get mixed up.

This chapter focuses on the role of the state as an employer, granting occupational pensions (public service pensions) to government employees. The study is limited to only one country: Norway. Occupational pensions in the Norwegian public sector have a longer history, and are more widespread, than occupational schemes in the private sector. Being older, they often served as role models when similar schemes were introduced in the private sector. Their institutional design also influenced tax and regulation policies vis-à-vis private sector occupational pensions: partly because regulators sometimes regarded public service pensions as an "ideal" type of occupational pensions, and partly because regulators often felt it difficult to deny tax privileges to private sector pensions, to the extent that they only provided the same benefits as the state awarded its own employees. The design of public service pensions even served as a point of reference in the public pension debate, concerning the question if and how the state should provide public superannuation, not only minimum pensions, for all its citizens.

What are the Problems?

A wide range of controversies surrounds the development of public service pensions. Some are undoubtedly nation-specific, having to do with the way public service pensions have evolved in various national settings. Others are presumably experienced by most countries which share a tradition of having established occupational pension schemes for civil servants or government employees, that is: almost all countries with a formalized state apparatus.

The chapter is built up around two questions. First: *What are the problems*? Second: What (in the eyes of Norwegian politicians) have been the solutions? To the extent that different countries perceive their problems in similar fashion, the various solutions should hold some general interest. If on the other hand countries perceive their problems differently, this might at least indicate to which extent our

15

perceptions are tied to the historical idiosyncrasies of the countries in which we live; it should sensitize us to the effect of our various national contexts on how we perceive our problems.

A Brief Outline of the Public/Private Pension Mix

As in most Scandinavian and Anglo-American countries, Norway has set up a basic (minimum) pension benefit financed out of general revenues. Norway has also introduced a public superannuation benefit, not unlike British SERPS. Unlike SERPS, however, there are no contract-out possibilities in the Norwegian superannuation scheme. On average, the superannuation system provides 60 percent of average earnings during the "20 best years" of a persons total life cycle income. 40 years of employment are necessary to earn a full superannuation benefit. An income ceiling in the public superannuation system implies that there is substantial room for occupational and personal pensions on top of the superannuation system[1]. The scheme is financed on a pay-as-you-go basis. The state, employers and employees share the costs (tripartite financing). Membership is mandatory both for employees and the self employed.

Occupational pensions, including public service pensions, top up public superannuation. Almost all state employees are members of a single defined-benefit occupational scheme, established in 1917. The scheme is financed on a pay-as-you-go basis. It provides 66 percent of final earnings if there is a service record of at least 30 years. Regional and local government employees are covered by their own occupational schemes. These schemes are fully funded, and there is some element of competition between insurance companies as regards the administration of the funds.

In the private sector, approximately 40 percent of all employees are covered by fully funded, company-based defined-benefit plans. Most private sector schemes also go for 66 percent of final earnings, and require 30 years of service to earn a full occupational pension.

In addition to occupational pensions, individuals may purchase pension annuities in the insurance market. The purchase of such annuities is widespread among the upper income strata and the self-employed. Individuals may of course also save for their retirement through other means. Investments in owner-occupied houses in particular may to some extent be retirement-motivated, as Norwegian tax laws employ a more liberal tax regime as regards investments in real estate than investments in financial assets.

As indicated in figure 1, the central government scheme has a dominant position within the public sector. 48 percent of all public employees belong to this scheme. Most remaining public service personnel (37 percent) belong to schemes administered by the insurance company KLP, which is mutually owned by those municipalities which allow KLP to run their schemes. Administering fully funded schemes, KLP has a total management capital of 60 billion NOK (approx. 10 billion US$) and is the fourth largest private owner of real estate in Norway (KLP Yearbook 1996:8,27). Separate pension funds, set up and run by local municipalities themselves, serve most of the remaining public sector employees.

These funds are mainly confined to the large cities; the Oslo municipal pension fund being by far the largest. Most private employees (among those who have access to occupational pensions) also belong to schemes administered by insurance companies. Some large employers (such as Norsk Hydro) operate their own pension funds. These funds are almost always set up as separate legal entities, with their own Board of Directors.

Figure 1. The Norwegian Public-Private Pension Mix, 1998

1. Basic pension (old age, disability, survivors) Flat-rate benefit financed from general revenues. Various means-tested benefits may supplement the basic pension.		
2. Public Superannuation (old age, disability, survivors) Approx. 60 percent of average earnings during "20 best years" with upper income limit.		
3. Public service pensions		**3. Private sector occupational pensions**
3.1. All employees employed by the central government. One unified pay-as-you-go scheme. 30 years of service to acquire a full pension. Approx. 66 percent of final salary.	*3.2. All employees employed by regional or local governments.* A multitude of funded schemes. Almost all plans mimic the central government scheme.	*3.3. 40 percent of employees in private sector.* Funded schemes. Most plans are more-or-less similar to the central government scheme.
4. Personal pensions and other individual savings instruments		

In the following, I focus mainly on the pension scheme serving central government employees (including teachers), and deal with the pension schemes serving regional and local government employees only to the extent that they deviate from the central government scheme. Being the oldest, the scheme serving central government employees has to some extent set the standards as regards public service pensions also in the regional and local government sectors.

Public Service Pensions in Collective Bargaining

Government service pensions were initially regarded as "gratification pay" provided by the employer (government) to its ageing servants. The practice of offering "after-pay" to civil servants too old or frail to fulfil their proper duties dates back to years prior to the establishment of a national Parliament in 1814 (that is: to the days of the Dano-Norwegian kingdom). This practice was upheld as

Norway came under the Swedish crown in the years 1814-1905. The present system was established in 1917, following the introduction of formal retirement ages in Norwegian public administration.

Parliament initially intended the 1917 scheme to be self-financed through a 10 percent compulsory contribution rate levied on employees (employees got a 10 percent wage increase in conjunction with the introduction of the scheme). However, in the years that followed, it became evident that this was not sufficient to finance benefits; not least since the new scheme allowed employees to include service records obtained before 1917. Gradually, the notion gained hold that public service pensions represent deferred wages, and that the contribution from the state represents an indirect wage cost. This principle was firmly established through a revision of the scheme in 1949.

Although government service pensions are officially regarded as part of wages, this notion has not fully sifted into the decision-making system surrounding public service pensions. Norwegian civil servants acquired the legal right to negotiate their salaries in 1933 (Sørensen, Underdal and Rasch 1990:92). Up till then, the salaries of civil servants were determined unilaterally by Parliament without formal consultations or negotiations. However, public service pensions were governed by a separate Parliamentary Act, rather than transferred to the wage negotiating arena. Consequently, each time the government, Parliament and/or government employees have wanted some amendment made, the stage has been set for a complex consulting and negotiating process between the Parliament, the Department of Administration (formally in charge of wage negotiations on behalf of the government), unions organizing government sector employees and in some cases even the courts in sorting out "who has the legal authority to decide what, with or without formal negotiations with whom", each time an amendment has been proposed. Thus Norway has not followed the Swedish lead to formally include government service pensions in collective bargaining between the state and its employees. Sweden made this change in the legal status of the scheme in the early 1990s.

The decision-making system surrounding occupational pensions among regional and local government employees (including medical personnel, who are employed by regional authorities in Norway) is less complex. These schemes are codified through collective bargaining arrangements rather than any Act of Parliament. However, the Department of Administration maintains some control also in the area of regional and local public service pensions. A separate set of regulations states that regional and local authorities are not allowed to negotiate an occupational pension deal with their employees which results in more generous pension benefits than those enjoyed by central government employees.

First Controversy: How to Split the Bill

What, then, have been the major political controversies surrounding public service pension schemes? The first and most basic controversy concerns how the government and its employees should split the bill. How large a proportion of salaries should be compulsory withheld from employees in order to finance their future pensions? In the 19th century, some MPs argued for the total abolition of public service pensions, and/or that employees should be compelled to pay all the costs (Overbye 1990:90-2) These MPs regarded government-sponsored payments to former civil servants as a "privilege" to be abolished. The 1917 legislation represented an attempt to make the scheme at least formally financed from employee contributions only. Also, the scheme was to be fully funded. However, since service records prior to 1917 were brought into account, the scheme almost instantly turned into a pay-as-you-go scheme. It also implied that the government had to continue to foot some of the bill.

Today, government employees pay 2 percent of their gross wage as a compulsory contribution to the scheme. The government pays "the rest". Since the scheme is pay-as-you-go and includes many rather complex co-ordination measures with public pensions proper, it is very difficult to assess how large the government share is. To complicate matters, the system involves a substantial amount of cross-subsidizing. Government employees with special (lower) pensionable age limits, such as the military and police force, pay the same contribution rate as others. Also, contribution rates are not differentiated according to differences in disability, survivor or longevity risks. This implies that indirect wage costs carried by the government on behalf of its employees vary between different groups of state employees, but not in any easily detectable way.

Second Controversy: Co-ordination with Public Pensions Proper

Norway introduced public old age pensions in 1936. As in most other Scandinavian or Anglo-American countries (except the US), the initial scheme was income-tested and financed from general revenues. Old-age pensions were to be reserved for those unable to contribute to their own pension; income maintenance in later years was regarded as a private responsibility.

In the following years, there was mounting pressure in Norwegian society to abolish the income test. The test was abolished in 1959 and the minimum benefit was replaced by a flat-rate basic pension. At the same time, Parliament decided that public service pensions were to be co-ordinated with the new basic pension, implying that their overall compensation level remained constant at 66 percent of previous earnings. This meant that the new flat-rate scheme in reality continued to be income-tested against one particular type of income: namely, income from the public service pension. To sweeten the pill, the contribution rate was reduced from 10 to 6 percent of gross wages, and state employees were not compelled to pay the full social security contribution levied on other citizens to finance the more generous old-age benefit (Orvin 1992). However, government employees close to or above pension age felt this co-ordination measure amounted to a partial confiscation of their savings and took the case to court. A High Court decision of 1962 ruled in favour of the state.

A similar controversy arose as Norway in 1966 decided to follow the Swedish example to top up the basic benefit with a public superannuation scheme. Again, the government decided to co-ordinate the new scheme with public service pensions, while bringing the compulsory contribution rate down from 6 to 2 percent of gross wages. Once more, this caused resentment among public sector employees, but the government had it its way.

The Norwegian story illustrates a more general phenomenon: Any attempt to increase the generosity of a public pension system involves conflicts with those who are served by occupational pensions. It might be worth while to contrast the Norwegian development with similar pension reforms in Sweden and Finland, which involved less intense controversies with public sector employees. Sweden introduced public superannuation in 1959. In the Swedish case, public employees had not been compelled to pay a percentage of their gross wage to finance their public service pensions (Overbye 1991:80-1). Instead, the government paid all of the costs. Hence less intense emotions arose as the government decided to co-ordinate the new public pension scheme with the existing public service scheme. As far as Finland is concerned, public earnings-related schemes were set up in 1960, but these schemes were reserved for private sector workers (Overbye op. cit.). In this fashion, the Finnish Parliament bypassed any controversies concerning how occupational pensions in the public sector were to be co-ordinated with new public superannuation schemes.

Without choosing side in the controversies which surrounded Norwegian co-ordination efforts, it should be noticed that public employees would have ended up with overall compensation rates close to, or above, 100 percent of previous earnings if their schemes had not been co-ordinated with the new public pension schemes. Hence co-ordination was in reality a precondition for being able to introduce broad-based public pension schemes in the first place[2].

Disagreements concerning co-ordination and contribution rates have by far been the most intense and politicized controversies surrounding public service pensions. Other controversies remain, but in these cases the debate has been less heated.

Third Controversy: Should All Government Employees Belong to the Same Scheme?

Initially, government service pensions were reserved for civil servants working full time. In the period 1917-1982, membership was gradually extended also to include part-time and temporarily employed personnel, other government employees than civil servants, and in the end also manual workers employed by the state. Thus since 1982 all employees who receive their pay check from the state belong to the same, unified government service scheme, and on equal terms. Part-time employees are included provided they work at least 15 hours a week, are employed for a duration period of at least 1 month, and end up with at least 5 years of accumulated public sector employment as they reach pension age[3].

Equity considerations have been the main driving force in bringing employees with rather different employment contracts into the same scheme. It was considered unfair that some state employees (notably civil servants) had access to a fringe benefit (public service pensions) which other employees serving the same employer (the state) were cut off from.

Even when public service pensions are formally a negotiated item of the wage package (as is the case in regional and local government plans), regulations imposed by the Department of Administration state that all employees must be included, and on equal terms[4].

Fourth Controversy: Vesting

Traditionally, occupational pensions in the public and private sector were considered a reward for long and uninterrupted service. The benefit could be lost if an employee left his/her employer or was dismissed. Over the years vesting rights in public service pensions have been steadily improved, and today these rights are better protected in public service pensions than in otherwise similar private sector occupational pension plans.

The employee earns a deferred benefit right depending on the number of service years relative to a full service record (30 years). Thus an employment record of 10 years as a general rule earns 10/30 of a full pension[5]. Pensions equal 66 per cent of final earnings provided there is a service record of at least 30 years. This is more generous than the public superannuation system, which requires 40 years of contributions for a full superannuation benefit. The deferred benefit is indexed in line with the so-called "base amount" (a core concept in Norwegian social security legislation). The base amount is not linked to any particular price or wage index, but is decided by Parliament each year after negotiations with various groups of social security recipients. Assumed to reflect changes in "prices as well as earnings", the base amount has traditionally been upgraded in between price and wage increases (Lorentzen 1987).

Fifth Controversy: Portability

State, regional and local government employees belong to different occupational pension schemes. However, government authorities have formed an agreement stating that occupational pension rights are transferable between state, regional and local government schemes. This implies that a state employee who moves to the municipal sector is credited with his/hers years of state service when entering the municipal pension plan and vice versa. This portability arrangement is made possible by the fact that almost all municipal pension plans imitate the design and benefit level of the state scheme; implying that a year of service in the state sector earns roughly the same amount of future pensions as a year of service in the regional or municipal sector.

There is no similar portability arrangement between occupational pensions in the public and private sector. Besides, as was illustrated in Figure 1, occupational pension coverage is more limited in the private than in the public sector.

Sixth Controversy: Benefit Levels

All Norwegian public service pensions are defined benefit-schemes. Unlike Denmark, where defined contribution schemes are widespread both in the public and private sectors, Norwegian employers in the public sector have stuck to the defined benefit-approach.

Pensions equal 66 percent of final earnings provided there is a service record of at least 30 years. However, only salaries above 8 times the so-called base amount (152 percent of average earnings in industry as of 1995) are calculated in full. Between 8 and 12 times the base amount only 1/3 of the salary earns a public service pension. Salaries above 12 times the base amount do not earn any public service pension at all. Contribution rates, however, are 2 percent of gross earnings without any upper limits[6].

A common critique of final salary plans has been that they discourage gradual retirement. If employees scale down their work effort at the end of their working career, rather than to quit permanently, they risk a reduction of their future pension level. To avoid this disincentive effect, special rules secure higher benefit levels to the extent that final salary should not be the year with highest salary. In this fashion, the scheme tries to encourage employees to maintain some presence in the labour market without risking a loss of pension benefits should they reduce work effort in the years immediately prior to retirement. Besides, no occupational pension benefit can be taken out prior to the age of 65 (except in the case of disability).

More recently, a debate has sprung up whether or not occupational pension schemes (including public service pensions) should be changed from defined benefit to defined contribution schemes. In a defined contribution plan, employees benefit from high interest rates on their contributions – but they also carry the risk if interest rates should for some reason turn negative in the future. Whereas in defined benefit plans, employees are *de facto* "insured" against future low rates of return (since their employer – in this case the state – is legally bound to provide a certain percentage of their final salary as a pension, regardless of interest rate developments in the contribution period). The price to pay for this insurance, though, is that the employer, rather than the employees, enjoys the benefit of higher-than-anticipated interest rates.

Deregulation of the Norwegian credit market during the 1980s, and the consequent surge in real interest rates, made Norwegian employees (including public employees) more willing to carry investment risk, i.e. willing to contemplate a shift from defined benefit to defined contribution schemes. In this respect, Norway is no different from other OECD countries, also marked by a strong interest in defined contribution schemes, following the world-wide deregulation of financial markets. However, this trend has been slow to spread to public sector pensions, not least since no one has been able to calculate the size of the contribution the state presently pays. Also a shift from defined benefit to defined contribution within public service pensions would make visible the substantial element of cross subsidy between various government sectors and agencies; and unions may be reluctant to open up this potential Pandora's box of conflicting interests among their members.

Seventh Controversy: Indexing

Public service pensions are indexed according to changes in the base amount. The indexation rule is similar to the indexing of public pensions proper, and different from indexation rules in private sector occupational plans. In the private sector, indexation of benefits depends on the return on the pension funds if the employer grants more than a nominal pension benefit in the first place, which is not always the case.

Eighth Controversy: Types of Benefits and Early Retirement Options

Public service pensions provide old age, disability and survivor's benefits. A disability pension is awarded provided there is a loss of work capacity of at least 25 percent. In this respect the Norwegian occupational pension sector (including public service pensions) is more generous than the public pension sector (minimum plus superannuation benefits), which awards a disability pension only for at least a 50 percent loss of work capacity. The retirement age was initially set at 70 years and this is still the age when an employer (including the state) may fire an employee without offering any reason other than mature age. The retirement age was lowered to 67 years in 1973. 67 years is also the retirement age in the public pension system. This is the highest retirement age not only in the OECD area, but among those 138 countries for which information on formal retirement ages is available (US Department of Health and Human Services 1992). Only Denmark and Iceland maintain a formal retirement age as high as Norway. Retirement ages are the same for men and women.

The high retirement age must be seen in the light of low unemployment rates during the 1970s and 1980s, which dampened popular demands for lower retirement ages or preretirement options. Also, the government has been reluctant to bring down retirement ages, anticipating a rise in pension outlays as the "baby-boom generations" reach retirement age between the years 2010 and 2030. However, in the late 1980s and early 1990s unemployment rates went up also in Norway, and there were increasing union demands for preretirement options. In the absence of government initiatives, the social partners agreed to set up a collectively bargained preretirement scheme (AFP) in 1992. This scheme extended the retirement option to the 66 and 65 age cohorts, at the same benefit level as in the public pension system. Public sector employees managed to negotiate a deal stating that they should also be granted the right to exit from their occupational pension scheme at age 65 without forfeiting benefits. Thus as of 1997, public service personnel are allowed to take out an occupational pension benefit equal to 66 percent of final salary from age 65.

In the years after 1992, AFP has been extended to encompass also the 64, 63 and 62 year olds. However, in these cases the retiree receives only the equivalent of his/her public pension. Public service pensions are not allowed to pay out benefits (apart from disability benefits) prior to the age of 65. In the private sector regulations are even stricter: no private sector occupational pension may start payments before the age of 67. Also, all benefits must be in the form of annuities: lump-sums are not allowed if the scheme is to enjoy tax privileges. Thus occupational pensions in Norway do not provide any incentive for retirement earlier than at age 65, unlike the situation in the US (cf. Lazear 1986).

Ninth Controversy: Funding Versus Pay-As-You-Go

The area of funding creates the starkest contrast between the central government scheme and the otherwise rather similar schemes serving regional and local government employees. The 1917 central government scheme is essentially pay-as-you-go. In the regional and local government sector, occupational pensions only became widespread after 1945. They were set up as fully funded schemes.

The administration of municipal pension funds are in the hands of three separate types of institutions. First, some large municipalities operate their own pension fund. Second, some municipalities allow a private insurance company to manage their fund. However, the most important administrator of regional and local government pension funds, including the large funds for medical personnel, is the insurance company KLP (established in 1949). KLP was – and is – mutually owned by those municipalities which at any given point in time allow KLP to administer their funds. Thus regional and local governments control the Board of Directors in KLP. This arrangement (which is also found among some insurance companies in the private sector) has its origins in pre-war "mutual fund" ownership arrangements.

During the 1980s and 1990s the government has been eager to increase the degree of competition in the pension insurance sector, to provide companies with an incentive to bring down administrative costs. This has led to controversies in particular in the municipal pension sector, as KLP employs somewhat different principles for the calculation of premiums than other insurance companies. There is a limited element of competition in this sector, as regional and local governments may leave KLP to allow another insurance company to administer its fund, or to set up a pension fund of its own. However, for various reasons few municipalities who once joined the KLP have so far actually taken the step to choose another administrator. 96 percent of all municipalities and regional governments still prefer KLP as the administrator of their funds (KLP Yearbook 1996:10)[7]. This might change in the future. Indeed, if insurance companies from European countries are allowed to compete on an equal footing within the European Economic Area (the EU plus Norway, Iceland and Lichtenstein), one might even conceive of a situation where KLP will face not only domestic but also European competition in the administration of regional and local government pension funds.

Tenth Controversy: Fund Management

As mentioned earlier, KLP has a total management capital of 60 billion NOK and is the fourth largest private owner of real estate in Norway. As is the case in other insurance companies, investments have gradually been directed away from government bonds and real estate toward the stock market, following a gradual softening of government portfolio regulations. Lending money back to municipalities (employers) has also been decreased.

Employers may be tempted to coerce fund managers to invest in their company, even if returns should be lower, and/or more risky, than other types of investment. This is a potential problem in particular in local pension funds. Employers might also have an interest in borrowing money from the fund at low interest rates, and/or to encourage the Board of Directors to invest in buildings which the employer may then rent at below-market rates.

To avoid intimidation of fund managers, Norwegian legislation states that the fund must be administered separately both from the employer (in this case: the municipality) and the unions, either in an insurance company or as a pension fund separated out as an independent judicial entity, with its own Board of Directors. There are limits on the amount of funds the employer and his/her employees might borrow, as well as the amount of funds invested in buildings rented by the employer. Also, all borrowing (and renting) should be at market rates. The Credit Inspection Agency has the role of supervising the return on capital, ensuring a "sufficient" dividend. Admittedly, effective monitoring and supervision might be difficult, especially in locally administered pension funds. Thus there remains some risk that employers may coerce the Board of Directors administering the fund to lend money back to the firm (or its employees) at below market rates without being detected, thereby weakening the fund. In this context, it should be noted that the Board of Directors of local funds have not (so far) been compelled to hire professional fund managers, although this is encouraged. At present, underfunding is a problem mainly in the few municipalities which administer their own pension fund (including the Oslo municipal pension fund, serving all employees employed by the Oslo city council). In some cases, local authorities have allowed these funds to slide toward pay-as-you-go schemes. This is partly due to a situation where the legal obligation on behalf of (politically elected) local councils to maintain fully funded occupational pensions has been somewhat more fuzzily defined than the legal obligation of an employer in the private sector to secure full funding. A recent (1996) government directive attempts to address this situation.

Although there might be certain problems in ensuring prudent investment of local pension funds, these problems should not be exaggerated. As long as the schemes are defined benefit with fixed indexing, employers know they will have to pay higher contribution rates in the future, if they are to forego high rates of return on today's funds. The problem – and thus the need for stringent monitoring and supervision – might possibly be more aggravated if employers have discretionary powers to determine the degree of indexing (as is often the case in private sector plans), or if schemes are based on defined contributions rather than defined benefits (as is customary in Denmark, but not yet in Norway).

Employers (including municipalities) may move their funds from one insurance company to another, or to a separate pension fund, providing insurance companies (in theory at least) with an incentive to keep down administrative costs and maintain high interest rates.

It is difficult to assess whether or not making municipal pension schemes funded rather than pay-as-you-go has had any effect on the overall national savings rate, or if the only effect has been on the composition of savings. No study has been undertaken to check out the pros and cons of this assumption.

Government Intervention in Private Sector Pensions

As mentioned in the introduction, the design of public service pensions has also influenced regulation policies directed toward private sector occupational pensions.

The government plays an active role in influencing the design of occupational schemes through a set of regulations tied to the tax code, as well as through mandatory laws. The private pension sector in Norway is dominated by company-based plans set up without formal negotiations with unions; rather similar to the US situation. The regulatory framework bears some resemblance to US ERISA regulations. However, Norwegian regulations provide employees with better vesting and portability rights than ERISA. Among the most important are:

1) All new employees who have been employed more than a year must be included, except for employees younger than 25, and employees with less than ten years of service left till they reach retirement age.

2) All employees working more than 50 percent of normal/full-time working hours, all seasonal workers employed more than 130 weeks in the last five years, or more than 20 weeks each year of these five years, must be included.

3) All employees who have been employed for 3 years or more must be given a deferred pension right if s/he leaves the firm. The deferred pension right must equal the contributions made by the employee, and by the employer on his/her behalf, in the period since s/he was employed.

4) In the (often long) period from the time the employee has left the firm till s/he reaches pension age, the deferred benefit must be kept in the pension fund, or in an equivalent fund, and be awarded the same interest as the fund. The employee may however take the deferred benefit with him/her, provided it is used as input in a personal pension plan.

5) Information as to the status of one's occupational pension rights must be made available on a regular basis, also to former employees.

Most of these rules were introduced after similar procedures had been established in public service pensions. During the 1980s and 1990s, the degree of favourable tax treatment of private (including occupational) pensions has been scaled back, although occupational pensions are still taxed somewhat more leniently than other types of financial assets. A recent Royal Commission Report (NOU 1998:1) suggests confining remaining tax subsidies even more closely to private plans where the benefit structure mimics public service pensions. If this recommendation is followed, Norway will continue to deny tax subsidies to defined contribution plans (as all public service pensions are defined benefit). As of 1998 defined contribution schemes have been introduced in Norway, but since they face a harsher tax regime they are few and far between.

Public Service Pensions and the Overall Pension Debate

As this chapter has shown, political controversies concerning public service pensions are many and multi-faceted. Dividing lines do not follow the traditional left-right axis in any clear cut manner. Adherents of different policies can even be identified within the major parties (the Social Democratic, Conservative, and Agrarian party). If one should none the less try to locate a cleavage line running through several issues, it would have to be the difference between what may loosely be labelled the "co-ordinators" versus the "deregulators" (although in practice, clear-cut proponents of one or the other view are hard to locate).

The "co-ordinators" want to integrate public, occupational and even individual/personal pension plans within an overarching regulatory framework. Public pensions are regarded as the basement, occupational pensions as the first floor, and individual pensions as the upper floor in a common pension-political "house". Public service pensions serve a crucial function within this frame of reference, since the pension level enjoyed by civil servants is often used as a yardstick for an adequate pension level. According to this line of thought, public service pensions represent a natural point of reference when assessing the adequacy of pension provision for other groups in society. Consequently, the role of various types of regulations and tax incentives should be to encourage other groups to aim for a pension level on a par with civil servants. In doing so, government regulations will simultaneously enhance a more standardized private (including occupational) pension sector.

On the other side one may pitch the "deregulators". According to their view, government responsibility should be limited to the provision of public pensions, be they generous or not-so-generous. Apart from that, the government should provide a neutral regulatory framework not only within the occupational pension sector, but also as regards the tax treatment of private pensions versus all other types of private savings. Regulations should leave the design of private pensions a private matter, to be decided within the households (with regard to individual savings instruments) or through individual or collective bargaining (with regard to occupational pensions). Public service pensions are perceived as "just another type of private pensions", reflecting nothing more than the particular current-versus-deferred-wages mix preferred by public servants. Within this frame of reference, a heterogenous private pension sector is to be encouraged rather than fought (assuming that people have different preferences with regard to current versus deferred life cycle consumption). This implies opening up the regulation of occupational pensions, allowing a larger diversity of schemes. These proposals would amount to a substantial policy shift with regard to public service pensions in particular, since these have traditionally been more standardized than similar pension schemes in the private sector.

In the past, Norwegian politicians have vacillated between these two points of view, without settling permanently for one or the other. A limited degree of deregulation has been pursued by various governments during the last decade in particular, but Norway has not gone "all the way" down the New Zealand path to a total opening up of the occupational pension sector – including public service pensions – to competition and scheme differentiation. Recent policy proposals may suggest a return to a more complex regulatory framework (NOU 1998).

On a more theoretical level, the never-ending vacillation between different policy approaches shows that the (historically derived) design of public service pensions remain an important institutional constraint on government policies in the pension area; both with regard to tax and regulation policies vis-à-vis the private pension sector, and with regard to the future fate of public superannuation. Public sector pensions served as a point of reference in the long period of welfare expansion characterizing the "first afterwar period" (1945-1989). In the present situation, characterized more by a "politics of retrenchment", public service pensions continue to serve as an institutional constraint on new policy initiatives. As long as the state provides its employees with occupational pensions, and in particular to the extent that these pensions are not fully integrated in the wage negotiating process, accusations that the state favours its employees above its citizens can be put forward if tax and regulation policies vis-à-vis private sector pensions are tightened up, and/or if public superannuation is scaled down. It may be that public service pensions have served, and continue to serve, as similar institutional constraints on policy also in other countries which provide government employees with occupational pensions. Having said that, it should be underlined that each country obviously has its own separate story to tell, with regard to the political controversies surrounding public service pensions; including how the existence of such pensions influence the larger debate concerning the relationship between public and private pensions more generally. My hunch, though, would be that these stories are variations on a common theme: a theme concerning how the three roles of the state in pension provision – as provider, regulator and employer – intertwine, and thus constrain policy makers in their attempts to pursue new, as well as old, policies in the area of pensions.

Notes

1. Only incomes up to six times the so-called "base amount" earn full pension credits. In between 6 and 12 times the base amount pension credits are granted for 1/3 of all incomes in this interval. Incomes above 12 times the base amount do not earn pension credits at all. In 1995, six times the base amount amounted to NOK 233082, or 114 per cent of average male wage in industry (Trygdestatistisk årbok 1996:22,24).

2. If the public service pension had been set up as a funded defined contribution rather than as a pay-as-you-go defined benefit scheme, it would not have been possible to co-ordinate the new public superannuation system with public service pensions. If this had been the case, the Finnish solution would probably have been the only available option also in Sweden and Norway.

3. Most regional and local government plans require at least 6 months continuous employment to grant a deferred pension right. 3 years of accumulated service is required at the end of the working career to earn a partial service pension.

4. The all-encompassing nature of occupational pensions within the public sector imply that these pensions are de facto more-or-less removed from collective bargaining also at the regional and local government level. Regional and local governments employ a heterogenous labour force, and employees belong to different unions. Employees may have different preferences as regards the mix between current and deferred wages. The clause stating that public service pensions are to encompass everybody, and on equal terms, imply that any single union is cut off from renegotiating the pension contract, unless all unions organizing municipal employees should agree between themselves to change the mix between present wages and future pension benefits in exactly the same fashion; which is hardly a realistic scenario.

5. The actual rule is somewhat more complex. The deferred benefit is to comprise the same proportion of a full pension as the relationship between accumulated years of service and the number of service years the employee would have accumulated from the year he was employed till retirement age, although this period is to be no longer than 40 years and at least 30 years (The Central Government Pension Service Act, paragraph 24.2). An example clarifies the rule: A 23 years old who quits his job 10 years later (at age 33) has 37 years left till he reaches the retirement age, which in this setting is 70 years. He thus receives 10/37 of a full service pension.

6. This suggests some element of cross-subsidy from high income to low income employees. Notice, however, that the public superannuation system is more generous toward low income than high income earners. This pulls in the other direction, and implies that low income earners benefit less from the top-up occupational pensions represent.

7. However, only comprising 65 percent of municipal and regional employees, since the largest municipalities usually operate their own pension fund.

References

Hippe, J.M. and A. W. Pedersen. *Når jobben betaler*. Oslo: FAFO-report no. 136, 1992

KLP. *Yearbook 1996*. Oslo: KLP, 1996

Lazear, E. Retirement from the labour force. In O. Ashenfeldter and R. Layard (eds): *Handbook of labour economics VII*. Amsterdam: North Holland, 1986

Lorentzen, H. *Verdiregulering av pensjoner*. Institute of Political Science, University of Oslo, 1987.

NOSOSCO. *Social Security in the Nordic Countries*. Nordic Social Statistical Committee report no. 5. Copenhagen: Nordic Ministry Council, 1996

NOU. *Utkast til lov om foretakspensjon*. Oslo: Norges Offentlige Utredninger, 1998

Orvin, H.W. *Statens pensjonskasse 1917-1992*. Oslo: Statens Pensjonskasse, 1992

Overbye, E. *God tjenestepensjon eller høy lønn?* Oslo: INAS report no.1, 1990

Overbye, E. *Offentlige og private pensjoner i Norden*. Oslo: INAS report no 10, 1991

Rikstrygdeverket. *Trygdestatistisk årbok 1986.* Oslo: Rikstrygdeverket, 1986

Sørensen, J., A. Underdal and B. E. Rasch. *Overordnet styringsinstans eller sideordnet part: Statens roller i inntektsforhandlingene.* Working Paper, Institute of Political Science, University of Oslo, 1990

US Department of Health and Human Services. *Social Security Programs Throughout the World – 1991.* Washington: Social Security Administration, 1992.

4 PRIVATIZATION OF PUBLIC SERVICE PENSIONS IN THE NETHERLANDS

Erik Lutjens

Introduction

The Dutch public service pension fund – the ABP Pension fund (Pensioenfonds ABP) – is the largest pension fund in the Netherlands, with over 80,000 active employees. With NLG 500 billion in invested capital, it is one of the largest funds in the world.

A public service pension fund has existed since the beginning of this century, although the ABP first came into existence at the beginning of the sixties. The ABP Pension Fund was then a fund established by law. The contents of the pension scheme were also laid down by law.

In the changing social environment, the system was found to be too oppressive and not sufficiently flexible. For this reason, privatization of the ABP Pension Fund was set in motion, with the result that since 1 January 1996 the ABP Pension Fund has been functioning as a private pension fund with a status equal to that of the trade and industrial sector pension funds for employees of trade and industry.

This paper examines more closely the reasons that led to privatization and the manner in which privatization has taken shape.

Reasons for Privatization

A complex of factors lies at the basis of the privatization of the ABP Pension Fund. The most important were:
1) the financial problems at the ABP had to be solved and
2) the government employers and the unions had to be given more freedom in negotiating the pension scheme.

2.1. Financial Problems

One of the reasons – perhaps the most important one – was that the ABP was no longer supposed to be dependent on the government with respect to financing of the pensions. Before privatization, fixing the premiums was the responsibility of the legislature. It is self-evident that where the legislature wore two hats – on the one hand employer, but on the other hand the guardian of public finances – the best choice was not always made for the financing of the pensions. From 1990 on, this led to the pension premium actually being fixed too low to meet future commitments. As from 1990, the supervisory body – the Insurance Board – has given negative advice on the premium transfer intended by the legislature, because it was too low. Nevertheless, the legislature persisted in its policy. The premium was lowered from 17.5% in the eighties to 8.8% in 1992. However, a premium to cover the costs at that time should have been fixed at between 16.6% and 19.5%.

Although the pensions of the ABP had to be financed with capital coverage, this low premium could be set nevertheless thanks to certain 'favourable' actuarial calculations. For instance, among other things, an optimistic – and, as it appeared later, too optimistic – estimate of the returns was assumed. At the same time, in the course of the years more insight was acquired into the administrative data, which resulted in a heavier valuation of the commitments. In addition, it was important that the public service pensions were indexed through linking with the public service salaries, and that since 1990 the commitments in this connection have increased sharply through inflation.

Negotiations between the Social Partners

A second reason for deciding to privatize was that more and more room became available for the government employers and the unions to have consultations on employment conditions, including the pension. However, before privatization, the contents of the pension scheme were laid down by law and there was not much to negotiate about. Also, every change to the pension scheme always had to be regulated by statutory amendment. This was also an inflexible system in which it was not possible to respond adequately to social changes which should have resulted in an adjustment of the pension scheme. Moreover, the negotiations tended more and more towards what is called sector consultation. In the statutory system there was a uniform pension scheme for all government employees, without distinction. Gradually, however, people began to realize that within the government and within the group of public servants as a whole, various separate sectors could be distinguished for which the employment conditions and pension scheme did not have to be identical.

The sectors distinguished are: central government, local authorities, provinces, water control authorities, police, judiciary and education. Each of these may have its own pension needs. For the police, for example, there may be more need for disability pension than for the judiciary. With privatization, the foundation has been laid for individual negotiations on the pension scheme and with that also for differentiation by sector.

The Privatization

The privatization of the ABP was therefore implemented and since 1 January 1996 it has been a fact. Through this the ABP has been organized as a private industrial sector pension fund, just like the trade and industrial sector pension funds for employees of trade and industry. The functioning of the ABP Pension Fund is no longer regulated by law, but falls under the private law regulations of the Pension and Savings Funds Act. This means that the 'usual' regulations that apply to pension funds also apply now to the ABP. These include:

- the obligation to provide capital coverage for the pensions. As such this was already applicable – see the foregoing – but the premium may now be determined by the Pension Fund itself;
- supervision by the Insurance Board. This entails, among other things, monitoring whether the degree of financing of the pensions is satisfactory.

Furthermore, the general rule applies that the ABP Pension Fund is an independent legal entity (legal person) with separate capital.

Contents of the Pension Scheme

Privatization has not yet resulted in any extensive changes to the contents of the pension scheme. The ABP has an indexed final pay scheme, with a pension for dependants and a disability pension. In 1996, a flexible retirement scheme was introduced as a novelty, in which people have the opportunity to chose to have their pension commence before the age of 65.

The expectation is that if the sector consultation on the contents of the pension scheme begins to acquire real significance (as from 1 January 2001, see also the following sections), a differentiation in the pension scheme might occur.

Mandatory Participation until 2001

Before privatization, mandatory participation in the ABP directly laid down by law applied to public servants. With privatization this statutory obligation has ceased to exist. It would, however, certainly be undesirable for the public servants to lose their statutory protection from one day to the next.

That is why the privatization Act contains a special transitional measure and a specific obligation has been laid down for the public servants to participate in the ABP Pension Fund. This special statutory obligation to participate is, as has been said, a transitional measure and it also has a limited period of effect, in this case until the year 2001.

Participation as from 2001

As from 1 January 2001 the special statutory participation will be converted by operation of law into mandatory participation in the ABP Pension Fund, pursuant to the rules of the Industrial Sector Pension Fund (Obligatory Participation) Act.

Under the aforementioned Act, the Minister of Social Affairs and Employment can make participation in an industrial sector pension fund mandatory (impose it as generally binding) for all employees in a specific industrial sector. This way, too, a special form of participation in an industrial sector pension fund is created which is mandatory under the law.

Exemption until 2001

Until 2001, no exemption from mandatory participation in the ABP will be possible for 'normal' government employees. A collective exemption is only conceivable for employees in the service of private institutions who were legally obliged to participate in the ABP before privatization. These institutions include those private institutions which carry out (quasi) governmental tasks, such as private hospitals. In order to obtain exemption from participation they must satisfy the condition that another pension scheme applies ant that the pension claims built up with the ABP are transferred to the other pension fund.

Exemption as from 2001

As from 1 January 2001 the situation at ABP will be different. The special statutory obligation to participate will no longer apply, but there will be – by legal definition – mandatory participation in an industrial sector pension fund. This implies that then the possibility of exemption under the Industrial Sector Pension Fund (Compulsory Participation) Act will also be in force. This possibility means that the ABP Pension Fund may grant an exemption to public servants if another equivalent pension applies. The exemption possibility concerns a power of the Pension Fund to grant exemption or not. There is no obligation to do so under the Act.

In addition to the possibility of exemption under the Act on mandatory participation, the Act on the privatization of the ABP Pension Fund has its own exemption possibility. It has been mentioned above that the privatization of the ABP Pension Fund laid the foundation for negotiating the pension scheme by sector and with that for setting up an individual pension scheme by sector. The Act on privatization of the ABP is in keeping with this because it stipulates that at the request of the employer in the sector and a representative labour union, the obligation to participate in the Pension Fund may be revoked for the sector in question. Such revocation is possible as from the year 2001.

Splitting up the Pension Fund?

As has been mentioned, the privatization of the ABP Pension Fund was also inspired by the idea that this would bring about more differentiation in the pension scheme, instead of the uniform statutory pension scheme as it applied before the privatization took effect. In particular, recognition of the possibility to negotiate the pensions by sector is expected to be put to actual use. In this way the sector can gear the pension scheme more to the nature of the work and the labour relations within the individual sector. The possibility described in the preceding section to revoke mandatory participation for an entire sector is also in keeping with the individual nature and individual need of a sector.

Sector consultation is expected to result in individual wishes for the pension scheme. A certain fear exists that this will be coupled with leaving the ABP and making use of the possibility to have mandatory participation revoked for an entire sector. If this does happen, in any case the ABP Pension Fund will lose some of its basis of support and therefore this is a matter of concern with a view to maintaining sufficient capital to finance the pensions of those who continue to participate in the ABP also in the long term. For the ABP as employer, concern about maintaining employment also plays a role.

It is not really necessary for a sector to leave the ABP Pension Fund in order to develop its own pension scheme. It is also quite possible for a separate pension scheme to be set up by sector within the ABP. Thus splitting up the ABP Pension

Fund is not the only possibility. The sector employers do have the possibility – but in joint consultation with the labour unions – through revocation of mandatory participation to leave the ABP Pension Fund and place the pension scheme elsewhere, for example with an insurance company. Mandatory participation for the sector employers as well will only apply fully until 1 January 2001. As from that date the system of a uniform public service pension scheme will be a thing of the past.

The Competitive Position of the ABP

After that date, however, the ABP will in principle have to compete with other insurance companies. The statutory monopoly of the ABP will disappear as a result of privatization. Until 2001 the ABP has the opportunity to prepare itself for the battle with its competitors. This demands a change of culture. Instead of being a quasi-public service organization in which the legal obligation to participate ensured that the product would be purchased, the ABP must offer something attractive to the sectors, because otherwise they will go to the insurance companies. The ABP is also preparing itself well for the year 2001. What can make the ABP attractive? A number of points:

- low operating costs. The ABP will have to work as cheaply as possible;
- service orientation;
- familiarity with government pensions, expertise;
- no loss of pension rights for employees who change to a job in a different sector;
- flexible possibilities.

With regard to the flexible possibilities, for some time the ABP organization as a whole has not been just a pension fund. The organization also includes an insurance company and a bank. In this way the ABP wants to be a multifunctional provider of services, to stay ahead in the battle with its competitors and in any case to win.

Conclusion

This paper has explained that an enormous change is taking place in the public service pension in the framework of the privatization of the Pension Fund for public servants, the ABP.

From the uniform mandatory pension scheme laid down by law, privatization has resulted in a scheme which may be established by the government employers together with the labour unions themselves. Furthermore, as from 1 January 2001 mandatory participation in the ABP for an entire sector (central government, local authorities, provinces, water control authorities, education, police, judiciary) may be revoked. It is to be expected that the uniform pension scheme for the entire government, for all public servants, will be a thing of the past. It is generally expected that the pension scheme will be differentiated by sector. Whether this will be coupled with splitting up the ABP Pension Fund because sectors choose to have their pension schemes administered outside the ABP (by an insurance company), or whether the ABP will administer a different pension scheme for each sector, will depend largely on how attractive the ABP is as a provider on the newly created free market.

5 FUNDING PUBLIC SERVICE PENSIONS IN DENMARK

Finn Østrup

Introduction

Based on the legal framework for employment, a distinction can be made between two groups of public employees in Denmark: (i) public servants (in Danish: tjenestemaend), and (ii) employees employed on the basis of collective wage agreements (in Danish: overenskomstansatte). The pension system differs between these two groups. We first discuss the scheme for public servants and next consider employees under collective wage agreements.

The Pension Scheme for Public Servants

A distinction can be made between the development of pensions for servants employed by the central government (the state) and the servants employed by the local government (the municapitalies, in Danish: kommuner).

While Danish kings often used pensions as a means to reward public servants, civil servants in the service of the state first became entitled to a pension with the adoption of the Danish constitution in 1849. The first law on pensions to civil servants, adopted by Parliament in 1851, laid down the principle that key groups of civil servants who retired due to age or ill health, were entitled to receive a pension, the size of which was determined by the number of years in service and by the size of the final salary. The widow of a civil servant became entitled to a pension while children below a certain age received children's benefits. While the right to receive a pension was originally limited to the key civil servants, defined as the civil servants who had received their appointment by the king, the pension right was gradually extended to broader groups of civil servants at subsequent revisions of the 1851 law. A reform in 1969 has made it possible for civil servants who change from public employment to the private sector, to maintain the pension rights which were acquired in the public sector.

Until 1958 it was left to the single municipality whether public servants should receive a pension. Most public servants had this right but provisions differed between municipalities. Through a revision of legislation in 1958, public servants in municipalities became entitled to a pension based on the same principles as the civil servants in the service of the state.

Pensions for public servants are financed through the public budgets. The development of the pension expenditure is shown in table 1. It can be seen that the expenditure has decreased as a percentage of GDP. The reason for this is the reduction in the number of public servants. An increasing number of public employees has chosen to opt for the status of employee under a collective wage agreement, cf. below.

Table 1. Public Expenditure on Pensions to Public Servants

	Public expenditure on pensions to public servants (percentage of GDP)
1975-79	0.94
1980-84	1.10
1985-89	1.07
1990-94	1.19
1995	1.19
1996	1.17
1997	

Source: Danmarks Statistik (Danish Statistical Office).

While pensions for public servants employed by the state are financed on a pay-as-you go basis, most municipalities pay a percentage of the public servant's salary to an insurance company, KP (Kommunernes Pensionsforsikring, in English: The Municipailities' Pension Insurance), which is jointly owned by the municipalities and by the professional association which includes the employees in the municipalities. In return, this insurance company has taken over the responsibility for the payment of pensions. KP was established when it turned out that many municipalities had not set aside adequate reserves to meet future pension payments. KP operates under the Danish Law on Insurance Business and is thus fully funded (see below).

Public Employees under Collective Wage Agreement

TheOpting-out of the Public Servant Scheme

Due to a low wage increase relative to other groups, the public sector found it increasingly difficult throughout the 1950s to attract staff, notably staff with a higher education. In 1959 this led to the introduction of a new legal framework for the employment of certain groups in the public sector, i.e. the status as employed under a collective wage agreement. For this new group of public employees, it was decided that pensions should no longer be financed out of the public budget on a pay-as-you go basis but should be financed through fully-funded pension funds managed by the members themselves, usually represented by the professional association for the group of public employees in question (see below).

One can point at several factors which may explain why it was decided to create separate pension schemes for the new group of public employees which were covered by collective wage agreements instead of continuing with pay-as-you go financing out of the public budget.

One explanation can be found in the smaller degree of transparency which exists with respect to pensions. In 1958, when the new status of employee under collective wage agreements was introduced, the main problem facing the public sector was difficulties in attracting staff, notably staff with a higher education. The status of employee under collective wage agreement was introduced to make it possible to give a large increase in compensation and thus to overcome the recruitment problems. To let part of the increase in compensation take the form of a contribution to a pension scheme was seen as a politically more acceptable way of granting the increase in compensation rather than opting for an outright salary increase.

Another explanation lies in the tax advantages associated with pensions provided through funded pension schemes. The Danish tax rules in 1958 granted full tax deductibility for contributions to pension funds. At the same time there was no taxation of the return on saving in the pension fund. These tax rules were of great importance in Denmark which is characterised by a high marginal tax rate on labour income and an effective taxation of capital income. This tax regime was especially important for high income groups, i.e. the groups which were first offered the status as employee under collective wage agreements.

The higher pension benefit which pensioners can expect to receive from the pension funds, is obtained at a cost for the government. If the pensions were alternatively financed from the public budget, the government could have reduced the government budgetary deficit and thus saved an interest expenditure and reduced government debt. The government accepted, however, this rise in the cost associated with pensions as the objective of the government was to attract key groups of employees by making it more attractive to work in the public sector. The tax advantages associated with pension saving in specialised pension funds made it possible with a given pension contribution from the public sector to achieve a large increase in the benefits which fell to the employee. This was seen as politically convenient as it involved less transparency concerning the true size of the increase in compensation which was granted to public employees.

A third factor behind the new pension regime can be found in the strong position of the Danish trade union movement. Through the establishment of pension schemes organised in special pension funds, the trade union for the groups of public employees took over a social responsibility for its members. There was a feeling among groups of high-income public employees that the task of providing for pensions would be more safely handled by special pension funds than having it financed through the public budget, implying a risk that the public sector could cut down on pension benefits especially to high-income groups.

At the same time, the consideration to strengthen the power of trade unions may also have played a role in the formation of pension funds which became closely related to the trade unions. The formation of special pension funds for each group of public employees further offered distinctive advantages to the trade union leaderships. Members of the trade union leaderships became members of the boards of the new pension funds.

A final reason behind the new pension regime was a desire in the Danish Finance Ministry to have greater transparency with respect to the public sector's future pension obligations. It was felt that there was little transparency with respect to pensions which were financed from the public budget and which would involve a future burden. By transferring the responsibility to pension funds, the government would not have to take account of a future increase in public expenditure, thus facilitating the management of the public finances.

The Expansion of Collective Wage Agreements in the Public Sector

Throughout the 1960s and the 1970s, the right to be employed under a collective wage agreement was extended to an increasing number of public employees. This caused a sharp increase in the number of employees under collective wage agreements relative to public servants (see Table 2). The group of employees under a collective wage agreement now comprises most staff who have received a higher education, e.g. doctors, economists, engineers, nurses, and teachers and most groups with employment in the social sector, e.g. social workers. Employees with the status of public servants now include mainly senior staff, e.g. directors in ministries, and employees in key sectors, e.g. defence and police.

Table 2. Number of Public Servants and Public Employees under Collective Wage Agreements

	Public servants in the state	Public servants in local government	Employees under collective wage agreement in the State	Employees under collective wage agreement in local government
1966	60,000	-	35,000	-
1970	65,000	-	37,000	-
1975	73,000	58,000	42,000	48,000
1980	68,000	73,600	50,000	59,400
1985	77,000	85,200	57,000	81,500
1990	81,400	86,800	58,800	108,200
1995	70,100	78,700	59,900	130,100

Source: Danmarks Statistik (Danish Statistical Office).

The growth in fully-funded pension schemes was promoted because the tax advantages associated with pension contributions became more important due to the rise in the marginal tax rate on labour income. In 1984, the tax advantages were reduced with the introduction of a tax on the return on pension saving, the so-called 'real interest rate tax', the objective of which was to leave a real return for pension savers corresponding to on average 3.5 percent. From 1999, this tax will be substituted by a flat-rate tax of 26 percent on all interest rate income in pension funds and a tax of 5 percent of the rise in share prices.

The Organisation of Pension Saving

The pension funds for public employees under a collective wage agreement have been organised on the basis of the professional associations which have negotiated the wage agreements. A separate pension fund has been established for a number of professional associations. There are at present 26 pension funds which cover different groups of public employees. There are for example established separate pension funds for roadmen, assistants at pharmacies, architects, social workers working with children and young people, engineers, veterinarians, doctors, etc.

The pensions are defined-contribution schemes. The schemes are further based on the 'equivalence principle', implying that the pension benefit received by a member on average corresponds to past contributions with the addition of the return which has been reached in the fund.

The composition of pension benefits received by a member depends on the provisions which have been adopted in each of the funds. In most funds, a full pension benefit can be paid out from the ages of either 65 or 67 years (in one fund full benefits can be reached from 60 years). At retirement at a lower age, a reduced pension benefit is paid out. Some funds have provisions which make it possible to have part of the pension benefit paid out as a lump sum from retirement. In the case of disability, a full benefit can be received before retirement. In the case of death, all funds grant a widow's pension, calculated as a percentage of the full pension benefit (for most funds 60 percent) and a benefit for surviving children (ranging between 20 and 25 percent of the full old-age pension benefit).

The funds are managed either by persons who are appointed by the professional association which has negotiated the wage agreement or by persons who are elected directly by the members. Most of these pension funds have their own administrations but some pension funds have created joint organisations for the management of the funds. For some groups of public employees, the municipal life assurance company KP manages the pension saving.

The pension funds come under the supervision of the Danish Law on Insurance Business. They are required to invest at least 60 percent of the funds in assets which are considered 'safe', most importantly government bonds and mortgage bonds while the remaining 40 percent can be invested in assets which are considered more risky, notably shares. To some extent pension funds have bought fixed property. Members of the pension funds have a priority when apartments in these houses are available. Pension contributions are tax-deductible while benefits are subjected to ordinary income tax. Lump-sum payments from the funds are taxed at a lower tax rate of 40 percent.

In the case where a person moves from the public sector to the private sector, the member can choose either to transfer the funds accumulated in the pension fund to a private sector scheme, or to maintain the saving in the pension fund, the member choosing to stop pension contributions. In the latter case, the member receives a reduced pension benefit at the time of retirement, the pension benefit being calculated in accordance with the 'equivalence principle' on the basis of past contributions with accrued return. The fully funded pension schemes based on the 'equivalence principle' are thus flexible when it comes to ensuring mobility between the public and private sectors.

Summary and Conclusion

This chapter has discussed the organisation of pensions for employees in the Danish public sector. One group of Danish public employees, the public servants, are entitled to receive a pension calculated as a percentage of the final salary. These pensions are financed from the government budgets. For another group of public employees, employment conditions are negotiated between the government and the professional association for the employees in question. For these public employees which come under collective wage agreements, the government pays a contribution to a separate pension fund which manages the funds. In this latter case, the pension benefit received by the member is calculated on the basis of past contributions with the addition of the return of the pension saving. Employment under collective wage agreement has become increasingly popular among public employees and this has led to a considerable build-up of pension funds for public employees. A number of reasons may explain why it was decided to transfer the responsibility for pensions to separate fully-funded schemes rather than continuing with finance out of public budgets. Most importantly, pension contributions were seen as a less transparent, and thus politically more acceptable, way of granting increases in the compensation of public employees. In addition, funded pension schemes have benefited from considerable tax advantages, the contributions being tax deductible while the tax rate on the return in the pension funds is lower than the tax rate for non-pension saving.

References

Friis, Poul Sorbye. *Historien om KP* (in English: The Story of KP). København: Kommunernes Pensionsforsikring, 1997.

Jensen, Carsten Vestero. *Det tvedelte pensionssystem* (in English: The Dual Pension System). Roskilde: Roskilde Universitetscenter, 1984.

6   THE DEBATE ON PENSION FUNDING FOR THE PUBLIC SERVICE IN GERMANY

Dagmar Kniep-Taha

Hiring, Ageing and Pension Costs

The future of the existing old-age provision schemes has come more and more under discussion in Germany. Like many other European states our country faces considerable changes in the age structure of the population. The overall demographic development requires all old-age provision schemes to introduce reforms designed to contain costs.

Having said this it cannot be denied that the special pension scheme for civil servants is facing particular problems. It is true that only one in three persons employed in the public service is a civil servant and the other two are so-called public employees who do not have the special status under the law governing civil servants' rights and duties. However, our 1996 Pensions Report has shown that the number of pensioners under civil servants law and with it the pension costs will rise particularly sharply. From here on I will therefore only refer to civil servants.

In principle, the rise in pension costs for civil servants does not differ in any way from the general problems of other pension systems. What is special about it, though, is that in the 1970s a lot of staff was employed because people expected the state to take on more and more tasks. Some of the characteristic campaigns launched at that time were: "Smaller classes", "Country areas to have their own secondary schools", "Two beds only in hospital rooms", "More law enforcement staff to step up the protection of internal security", "Reduction of working hours". The pension benefits for the civil servants taken on for these measures now need to be financed.

The effects on the pension situation come up 35 to 40 years later: In 2010, the German territorial authorities will have to pay pensions for just above one million civil service pensioners, while in 2020 there will be 1.27 million pensioners. The peak will be reached in 2023 with 1.29 million. Only afterwards the number will go down slowly to the 1 million level by 2040.

Pension expenses are not only determined by staff numbers, though. Firstly, the qualification and pay of staff has risen, and secondly the overall periods during which pensions are drawn have gone up. This is not primarily due to increased life expectancy, but to the fact that civil servants in Germany retire on average at the age of 59 and thus six years before reaching the statutory age limit.

Having said this we also need to look at public pension expenses in their context. The loyalty relationship existing between civil servants and their state employer is a special one established for life. Therefore the pension only reflects the employer's continued obligation to ensure their maintenance. Pension expenses are therefore shown as a part of the overall staff costs in the public budgets.

Implicit Employee Contributions

From a financial point of view, too, the pension differs from the statutory basic pension system, in which the ratio of the number of contributors to the number of recipients is instrumental in determining the contribution rate and where therefore it is desirable to have as many contributors as possible. In the civil servants' pension scheme pay and pension go together, which is why other mechanisms are at work. Civil servants are excluded from the statutory basic pension scheme and do not pay any contributions towards their pension which appear as such. Instead, the overall costs, i.e. in particular the pension-costs, are already taken into account when determining the amount and structure of civil servant pay. This is also true for the regular pay adaptations.

Economically the pensions are based on retained pay elements which do not officially appear in any pay slips, which means that the pay of active civil servants already takes into account their subsequent pension entitlement. The fact that the pay is determined so as to take into account future pension benefits means that civil servants indirectly accept a lower pay.

Thus, civil servants contribute to their old-age provision. In future, however, this will not suffice in order to fairly distribute future burdens on the whole society on the one hand and on the public service on the other. Public service pension burdens will peak in the years 2020 to 2025. Therefore the Federal Government, at the suggestion of the Federal Minister of the Interior, has newly introduced some special statutory pension reserves. Under this reserve-concept, the pay and pensions of civil servants will not be fully adjusted to the collective wage agreement for public employees for a longer period, so that civil servants and pensioners will make an additional implicit contribution towards the cost of coping with the problems of providing for old-age pensioners in the public service.

If civil servants' pay and pensions lag behind the annual wage agreements by 0.2 per cent for fifteen years, they will *permanently* be reduced by 3%. After these 15 years the reserve including the interest accrued will amount to far more than 60 billion Marks. Later on the money will be used to contain pension expenses so that the overall economy is not stretched too far even in peak periods.

The decisive aspect is that this statutory reserve is funded exclusively from savings made through pay losses – and not from publicly borrowed money – and is therefore exclusively designed for the pensions provision of the persons concerned.

Funding

This funding of the reserve through a loss in pay of the persons concerned is what mainly distinguishes it from fund models launched by some Federal *Länder*, which are fed from publicly borrowed money.

Let me briefly go into the budget law situation:

Civil servants' pension benefits are paid directly from the current budget and thus from current tax revenues. They differ from pension payments made under the statutory basic pension scheme: Statutory pensions are paid for by current contributions made by the active workers *and* by the employers, while pension benefits for civil servants are paid for only by the public employers.

In actual fact, though, both schemes work on a pay-as-you-go system where, leaving aside minor liquidity reserves, no surpluses and no stocks of capital can be accrued which could be used to pay out benefits.

That means that even the statutory pension insurance system is not based on a funding principle – contrary to what some people in Germany are led to believe by the actual term "statutory pension *insurance*". It is only in the case of private annuity insurances and life insurances that the contributions accumulate a profitable capital stock the proceeds from which are used to pay out the benefits. It is obvious that these private schemes need to build up reserves simply because it is not guaranteed that the insurance institution will continue to exist nor that the number of persons having to make contributions will remain the same. In contrast, it is safe to assume that the state institutions paying out benefits will continue to exist and that there will always be a sufficient number of tax payers.

However, the differences are not as great as they may appear at first sight. While the pay-as-you-go system relies on the long-term and stable wage efficiency, the capital stock system is hinged on the efficiency of capital incomes. In the final analysis, this means that in both cases current pensions always have to be taken from current real net output produced by the current gainful population either by contributions and/or taxes.

Obviously, any fund, bank or insurance can only pay interest or distribute profits if there is someone in the first place who productively invests or manages the savings which have been paid in, i.e. who achieves results, makes profits and from these profits pays interest charges to the bank or insurance company, or dividends to the fund. If that is so, it is not possible, from an overall economy point of view, to bring about a shift in income for the whole society with a time delay. It is only possible to fund a shift in income from the current Social Product between two groups existing at the same time.

What we learn from this is that there is no funding system which could abolish real changes in burden caused by demographic changes. What we need to solve pension problems in Germany is not exchanging the system, but an adjustment of the current system.

It is against this background that the "pension funds" set up by the two German Federal *Länder* Schleswig-Holstein and Rheinland Pfalz in 1995 have major deficiencies. Both *Länder* have built up special funds, which, in the final analysis, are fed from credit financed means, i.e. money borrowed by the public employers. Not only does this solution cause additional administrative effort. Also, it fails to make real "provision" for the future. This is so for the following reasons:

Firstly, fund means are taken from the current state budget, i.e. to put money aside which is urgently required today. This is breaching the principle that, where budget deficits are chronic, financial means may only be obtained if and when they are actually needed and may not be used to partially cover costs which will incur at a much later time.

It is a well-known fact that money can only be earned and spent once. There is no economic advantage to using this kind of pension fund. Since it does not increase the bottom line the idea seems to be no more than "hot air" in the books.

In this context it does not make more sense if the *Land* is going to borrow money from the fund. But that is what Schleswig-Holstein and Rheinland-Pfalz have in mind: As long as benefits are not paid from the fund the amounts "saved" shall be made available to the *Land's* purse on the terms and conditions prevailing on the market – i.e. as an interest-bearing loan. In other words, the *Land's* purse borrows money from a fund which it has filled with borrowed money to begin with[1]. Any housewife knows that the interest earned for the money in a savings account is always lower than debtor credits. I think that no more needs to be said about such an "internal cycle of payment flows".

And the two *Länder* have to pay twice: once for the money borrowed to feed the funds and once again for the money borrowed *from* the funds. More than that, all this has to be paid from the ever tighter public budget on top of having to finance increasing pensions. Thus, the *Länder* face an unnecessary extra burden for decades.

The Federal Government in Germany has repeatedly pointed out this *problème de passage*. The case of Schleswig-Holstein illustrates that this burden cannot be borne for long: It was less than two years after the establishment of the funds that the fund "assets" were ingloriously re-incorporated into the overall budget in Spring 1997. The reason given was as laconic as it was foreseeable: the funds means were required for the current budget, and the costly reserves could no longer be afforded.

This experiment shows that credit-funded reserves to finance the pensions for civil servants is not useful from an economic point of view because the refinancing costs are bound to exceed the interest borne by the special assets built from the reserves.

Therefore the only fund concept which is recommendable is one which is pursued parallel to the existing pay-as-you-go system and where annual amounts are paid in which can be afforded without credits. This is the course the Federal Government in Germany intends to take: It does not seek to adopt another system, but to cut back the pension expenses in the peak period between 2020 and 2030. The money is to be paid in stages and contributed by civil servants and pensioners. Obviously, this fund contains real "savings" coming from and belonging to the civil servants and pensioners. Of course the capital also bears interest because it may be borrowed by the public purse on the terms and conditions prevailing on the market.

This system also ensures a social and fair treatment of those concerned. It is above all in the field of old-age provision that pensioners have to be able to rely on the arrangements which they have prepared for during their last working years. The burdens which we will undeniably have to face will be borne in the public service by the active staff and the pensioners together. Accordingly, the contribution is so low that it will amount to only a small part of the future annual increases. Let me just mention at this juncture that the statutory pension insurance in Germany has submitted a plan which is very much like the above concept: a so-called demographic factor is to be included in the calculation formula. The result is that annual increases will be a little less in the future so the level of statutory pensions is slightly lowered in the long run.

Let me conclude by giving a quote which is increasingly mentioned in the discussion going on in Germany about the establishment of old-age pension funds for civil servants: "It is more likely for a dog to stock sausages than for politicians not to spend available money".

Obviously it seems to be almost impossible to guard against the action of all future legislators. Therefore the administration of the fund assets is not only regulated by law and is not only subject to the Ministry of Finance. In addition, the investment and use of the funds is controlled by an independent advisory board on which there are above all representatives of the occupational associations of civil servants. I assume that that way it will be possible to protect the civil servants' fund assets also from future governments.

The earlier the necessary measures will be introduced the less the effects will be felt by the individual civil servant and the greater the success in shaping the civil servants' pension system in line with the requirements the future holds.

Notes

1. The result would not be any different if the pensions were funded from short-term budget surpluses, for instance from the sale of public enterprises. These could no longer be used to repay debts; the loss in interest which would not have to be paid is almost equivalent to the interest earned through the special assets.

7 REFORM OF PENSIONS FOR FEDERAL GOVERNMENT EMPLOYEES IN THE UNITED STATES

John A. Turner and David M. Rajnes

Introduction

In 1983, the United States reformed the retirement program covering most federal government employees. The Civil Service Retirement System (CSRS) was closed to new members and all new federal government employees were required to join the new system, called the Federal Employees Retirement System (FERS). This reform succeeded in partially privatizing the provision of retirement income to federal government workers and over the long run will reduce the unfunded liability associated with the retirement benefits of federal workers.

Members of the old system were given the option of switching to the new system, but only 2.8 percent did. It was generally felt that the new system was better for workers who intended to leave the federal government before retirement, but that the old system was better for workers who intended to stay with the government.

Because few workers switched from the old system to the new one, these two systems coexist and are by far the largest retirement systems for federal government employees. The two programs each now cover nearly half of the 2.8 million active federal civilian employees not covered under other federal retirement systems – 1.375 million under FERS and 1.443 million by CSRS at the beginning of FY 1995. Several small systems cover the remaining federal employees, including such groups as diplomats (State Department), spies (Central Intelligence Agency), and central bankers(Federal Reserve Board), but contain relatively few employees.

This chapter explains how the two systems work, why the reform was done, and what implications the reform has for workers and the federal budget.

The Civil Service Retirement System (CSRS)

A major feature of the CSRS, the "old" system, is that employees covered by that system are not covered by social security. The CSRS was started in 1920 and thus predated the social security system, which began in 1937. When social security was enacted, federal government workers were excluded from its coverage. Before the reform in 1983, federal government employees were the largest group not covered by social security. The program is projected to end about 2070, when the last beneficiary of the system is expected to have died.

CSRS allows employees with 30 years of service to retire at age 55 with unreduced benefits. Most employees either do not have 30 years of service at that age or elect not to retire when first eligible. The average CSRS retirement age is 61.5 (U.S. GAO 1995). This is also the average age of retirement for the general population.

The CSRS provides a price indexed retirement benefit. In order to reduce government expenditures so as to reduce the budget deficit, a number of cost-saving changes have been made to the cost-of-living adjustment (COLA) for CSRS. Nonetheless, the CSRS has provided nearly full inflation protection. US General Accounting Office computations indicate that the COLA delays and reductions during the decade from 1985 through 1994 resulted in COLAs for CSRS equal to 80 percent of the CPI increase during that period (US GAO 1995). This is better protection than provided in nearly all nonfederal plans. It is less, however, than the inflation protection provided through social security. Most workers in private sector jobs equivalent to employment in the federal sector are covered by occupational pension plans, but these plans never provide full inflation indexation. Considering the full inflation protection private sector workers receive through social security and the partial inflation protection they receive through private pensions, upper income federal workers had better inflation indexation of retirement benefits than was available for private sector workers, while low income federal workers had worse inflation protection than the full inflation protection provided lower income workers through social security.

Federal Employee Retirement System (FERS)

The Social Security Amendments of 1983 brought all new federal civilian employees hired after December 1983 into the social security system. This change was primarily intended to help solve the short run financing difficulties of social security by bringing more contributors into the system, with no increase in social security benefit payments for many years.

Inclusion of federal government employees in social security necessitated restructuring of their retirement income benefits. The structure of FERS was determined after study of private sector retirement benefits. The change was not the result of bargaining or consultation with federal employees but was the result of legislative changes proposed by the executive branch of government and enacted by the Congress.

FERS was designed so that it would provide retirement income comparable to that provided by large employers. In the private sector, all workers are covered by social security. Most large enterprises, which would be comparable employers to the federal government, offer their employees a defined benefit plan and a supplementary defined contribution plan. FERS adopted this approach, providing a three tier retirement plan. It provides federal workers coverage under social security, a defined benefit plan, and the Thrift Savings Plan (TSP), which is a defined contribution plan.

FERS employees pay full social security contributions. In addition, they contribute 0.8 percent of pay to the Basic Benefit Plan, which is the defined benefit plan. Few private sector employers require employees to contribute to their defined benefit plans because this contribution is not tax deductible while employer contributions are tax deductible.

In addition, the worker's agency contributes an amount equal to 1 percent of pay into the worker's Thrift Savings Plan account. Workers can make tax deferred contributions to the TSP, and a portion is matched by the Government.

The FERS basic benefit plan, being only one portion of a three-part retirement system, has a considerably lower accrual rate than the CSRS plan. The CSRS plan has accrual rates of 1.5 to 2 percent per year of service (increasing with years of service), while the FERS plan has accrual rates of 1.0 to 1.1 percent per year of service.

The FERS plan provides substantially reduced retiree cost of living adjustments (COLAs) compared to the nearly full COLAs provided by the CSRS. FERS retirees do not receive COLAs until age 62 – an incentive to postpone retirement until age 62 – while in the CSRS COLAs are available at retirement, which could occur 7 years earlier, at age 55. The FERS COLA provides full protection up to an inflation rate of 2 percent. For inflation of 3 percent or more, it equals the increase in the Consumer Price Index (CPI) less 1 percent. The FERS plan thus provides less inflation protection than does the CSRS plan. FERS retirees, on the other hand, receive full inflation protection for their social security benefits(US GAO 1995).

Workers retiring before age 62, which is the first age when social security benefits are available, receive an annuity supplement until age 62 that equals the estimated social security benefits that the retiree could have earned while employed by the federal government upon retiring at age 62.

Thrift Savings Plan

The Thrift Savings Plan offers federal workers the same type of savings and tax benefits that many private corporations offer their employees under 401(k) plans. 401(k) plans are by far the most popular type of defined contribution plan for private sector workers. By participating in the TSP, workers can save part of their income for retirement, receive matching government contributions, and reduce their current taxes. The TSP is the part of federal retirement income that the worker can control because the worker decides how much of pay to put into their thrift account, how to invest it, and, when they retire, how to receive the money.

As of December 1996, this plan had assets of $46 billion, making it, after roughly a decade's existence, one of the 20 largest pension funds in the United States. With average daily growth in assets of $27 million, it is projected to become the largest U.S. pension fund.

The plan is administered by an independent government agency, the Federal Retirement Thrift Investment Board, which is charged with operating the plan prudently and solely in the interest of the participants and their beneficiaries.

In the Thrift Savings Plan, like 401(k) plans in the private sector, workers contribute before-tax earnings. For FERS employees, the federal government automatically contributes one percent of pay. Workers in FERS may contribute up to 10 percent of pay. For workers who choose to contribute, the federal government matches their contribution up to 5 percent of pay – dollar for dollar for the first three percent and 50 cents per dollar for the next two percent, for a maximum government contribution of 5 percent of pay, and a maximum total contribution of 15 percent.

The 15 percent maximum contribution is relatively high. For example, it compares favorably with the 10 percent of pay that workers in the Chilean pension system contribute towards their retirement. In 1990, 76 percent of male and 62 percent of female eligible federal (FERS) employees contributed to the Thrift Savings Plan.[1] Of the 2.2 million participants in the plan in 1996, 1.7 million contributed their own money (Arthur Andersen 1997). Thus, a sizable portion of the FERS employees do not take advantage of the government match. This lack of participation is a concern. Years later, workers not having made voluntary contributions may feel they have inadequate retirement income.

While the accumulated funds in the Basic FERS plan, CSRS and social security, are all invested in Treasury securities, the Thrift Savings Plan has several funds in which participants may invest. Workers can invest any portion of their contributions into any of three investment funds and can transfer any portion of their account balance among the three funds.

The G fund holds short-term U.S. Treasury securities specially issued to the plan. The F fund contains both government and corporate bonds. This fund is invested in a bond index fund, the Barclay's U.S. Debt Index Fund, that tracks the performance of the Lehman Brothers Aggregate bond index. This index consists primarily of high quality fixed income securities representing the U.S. Government, corporate, and mortgage backed securities sectors of the U.S. bond market. The C fund is currently invested in the Barclay's equity index fund, a Standard & Poor's (S&P) 500 index fund that consists of the common stocks of all companies represented in the S&P 500 index. The Barclay's Equity Index fund is a commingled fund with $56 billion in assets at the end of 1996, of which approximately half were assets of C fund participants and half were assets of other investors. While this fund is riskier than the other two funds, it is well diversified and thus much less risky than investing in individual company shares. The investment managers of the C and F funds are changed periodically, as new investment management contracts are competitively awarded by the Thrift Savings Board.

Both the F and C funds are passively managed, meaning that the investment choice is automatically dictated by an index. Passive management involves less trading and lower investment costs than does active management, where the investment manager actively trades securities, attempting to determine the best time to buy or sell individual securities.

The three funds allow workers, if they wish, to invest in stocks when they are young and then switch to bonds as they approach retirement. Participants can make an interfund transfer in any month with no annual limitation.

Presumably reflecting the risk aversion of government workers, the funds of the Thrift Savings Plan are invested primarily in government securities. At the end of 1996, 52 percent of the total investments in the Thrift Savings Plan were in the U.S. government securities fund, 43 percent were in the common stock fund and 5 percent were in the fixed income fund.

Two additional funds, an international fund and a small cap fund (investing in small businesses), have been approved to provide investment outlets to members of the Thrift Savings Plan. These funds will be available to participants in about the year 2000.

Record keeping for the Thrift Savings Plan is provided through a contract with the Department of Agriculture's National Finance Center (NFC). The NFC fees for 1997 are estimated to be $27 million, or roughly equivalent to one day's increase in the assets of the TSP. In 1996, the overall administrative expenses of the Thrift Savings plan were $39 million dollars, which is 0.1 percent of beginning year assets or roughly $20 per participant per annum.

These expenses do not include investment expenses. In 1996, plan expenses allocated to the G fund reduced its rate of return by 0.08 percent. Plan administrative expenses and investment management fees reduced the rate of return on the F and C funds by 0.1 percent and 0.09 percent. These administrative expenses do not include the expenses of federal agencies in collecting and transmitting the funds to the Thrift Savings Plan, but that type of expense is usually not included when measuring administrative expenses of pension funds.

The expenses also do not include the trading costs of the C fund. However, because of the large asset size of the investment manager of the C fund, many C fund purchases of stock units are exchanged with the units of other clients who are selling stocks, in which case no fund trading costs are incurred in financial markets. For this reason, the overall trading costs of the C fund are very low.

When compared to contributions, the administrative expenses are roughly 1 percent of contributions, which is about the same level of administrative expenses as reported by the U.S. Social Security Administration.

Administrative expenses are prorated equally across all invested assets. Because administrative expenses tend to be largely fixed costs, this pattern redistributes income from workers with large accounts to those with small accounts.

Other Provisions under the FERS System

The minimum retirement age under the FERS plan depends on the year of the worker's birth. Workers born before 1948 can retire at age 55 with sufficient years of service. Workers born in 1970 and later can retire at age 57, and workers born in the intervening years have minimum retirement ages between age 55 and 57. Workers who do not meet the requirement of 30 years of service can retire at age 60 with 20 years and age 62 with 5 years. In addition, workers can retire at their minimum retirement age with 10 years of service at a reduced benefit. In case of forced early retirement due to a major reorganization or reduction in the workforce, workers can retire at age 50 with 20 years of service or at any age with 25 years.

The basic benefit is based on the worker's "high 3 average pay," figured by averaging the highest basic pay over any 3 consecutive years of service. The benefit is calculated as 1 percent of the high 3 average pay times years of service, so that a worker with 30 years of service would receive 30 percent of their high 3 average pay. In addition, workers who retire at the minimum retirement age with 30 years of service or at age 60 with 20 years receive a special supplemental annuity, payable until age 62 when they begin receiving their social security annuity.

Comparison of the Two Systems

For career workers, in several ways the FERS system is a less generous system than the CSRS system. This is reflected to some extent in Table 1. Workers born in 1970 and later have a minimum retirement age under FERS that is two years older than that under the CSRS. However, under FERS employees may retire with reduced benefits at age 55 to 57 (depending on their birth year) with 10 years of service.

The cost of living adjustment is also less generous under FERS. While there is in most years a nearly full cost of living adjustment under the CSRS, under FERS the cost of living adjustment does not start until age 62 and the adjustment is less than full.

For workers who do not plan to work in the federal government for an entire career, the FERS system provides better portability of benefits than does the CSRS system and better benefits for workers entering the government later in life. Thus, the FERS system may be better for mobile workers. The benefits in the TSP and benefits accrued under social security are fully portable in the FERS system. By contrast, workers in the CSRS system suffer large portability losses, much larger than those suffered by workers in the private sector, because they do not benefit from the portability of social security. It has been argued, for example, that the low quit rates of federal employees before the FERS scheme was created, reflected the large capital losses that would be imposed by the government on workers who quit before retirement (Ippolito 1987).

Issues in Retirement Policy Towards Federal Government Workers

This section considers several issues concerning policy towards retirement of federal government workers.

Retirement Age. The Civil Service Retirement System has been criticized for providing benefits at 55 years old, which is 7 years earlier than social security provides retirement benefits. Because of the 30-year service requirement, most federal employees do not qualify for retirement at age 55. On average, the employees retiring in fiscal year 1994 were 61.5 years old and had 30 years of service. About 35 percent were retirees between the ages 55 and 59, averaging 57 years of age and 35 years of service (US GAO 1995).

Legal Protection. Civil servants in the federal government participating in federal retirement plans do not receive the protection of the Employee Retirement Income Security Act of 1974 (ERISA), which protects all private sector employees. ERISA protects private sector employees from reductions in their accrued benefits. By contrast, there is no such protection for federal government employees, whose benefits can be changed at the discretion of Congress.

Table 1. Comparing the Major Sub-Systems of the US Civil Servant Pension Scheme

Feature	Civil Servant Retirement System (CSRS)	Federal Employee Retirement System (FERS)
Contributions	Employee 7% of basic pay matched by government	Employee: 6.2% for OASDI plus 0.8%; government: about 12.9%
Eligibility for full annuity	Age 55 with 30 years of service; Age 60 with 20 years of service; Age 62 with 5 years of service	Age 55 with 30 years of service; Age 55-57 for employees born between 1948-70; Ages 60 (62) with 20 (5) years of service
Benefit formula	Wage base: Highest 3 years average; Accrual: 1.5% times first 5 years, 1.75% times next 5 years; 2% times service beyond 10 years up to 80% of average salary	Wage base: Highest 3 years average; Accrual: 1% or 1.1% at 62 with 20 years service (replacement of 40-44% after 40 years of service)
Pension indexation	Full price inflation (CPI)	None before 62 for most employees; full CPI at 62 if CPI less than 2%; 2% if CPI is 2-3%, and 1% below CPI if CPI above 3%
Involuntary/Early retirement	Any age with 25 years of service or more; Age 50 after 20 years of service(benefit reduced by 2% a year for each beginning before age 55)	Unreduced benefit: at any age (age 50) after 25 years (20 years) of service; Reduced benefit: after 10 years of service
Refund options	Choice of lump-sum withdrawal of contributions when leaving	Option to withdraw contributions in lump-sum when leaving and will receive no annuity
Disability benefit eligibility	Must have at least 5 years civilian service	Requires at least 18 months of service; worker must apply to FERS & social security
Survivor eligibility	Requires at least 18 months of civilian service	Requires at least 18 months of service
Thrift Savings Plan (TSP)	Voluntary; may contribute up to 5% of pay without matching government contribution	May contribute up to 10% of pay with federal matching (automatic 1%) up to 5%
TSP: Optional loan	May borrow from own contributions to TSP plans for any purpose; designated repayment period	May borrow from own contributions to TSP for any purpose; designated repayment period
Options for TSP benefits	Annuity for life or fixed term; lump-sum payment at retirement or death; or may transfer fund to IRA when leaving government service	Annuity for life or fixed term; lump-sum payment at retirement or death; or may transfer fund to IRA when leaving government

Source: 1995 Federal Personnel Guide and US GAO 1996

Funding. Most federal government pension plans are underfunded. However, FERS is considered fully funded or nearly fully funded under different actuarial measures, and statutory provisions for the future elimination of the unfunded benefit obligations of the CSRS have been enacted.[1] It must be realized that federal retirement benefits are not prefunded in the way that private pension plans set aside money during employees' working years to cover the accruing costs of these benefits, because the plans' assets are largely invested in special issue nonmarketable Treasury securities available only to the retirement funds. Resources must be available – either through general tax revenues or borrowing – when the securities are redeemed to pay retirement benefits, and, to the extent that borrowing becomes necessary, this action will add to the deficit.

CSRS and FERS funding use a "normal cost" approach, or the set aside of a percentage of payroll during employees' working years that, with investment earnings, should be sufficient to cover future benefit payments. The CSRS approach, unlike that used in the FERS scheme, calculates future costs without factoring in either COLAs or pay increases. Under the FERS system, agencies are required to contribute this extra amount to bridge the gap between expected costs and employee contributions.

Because of the manner in which the CSRS costs are determined and funded, the system has accumulated a sizable unfunded liability. According to the US General Accounting Office, the unfunded actuarial accrued liability of both CSRS and FERS equaled $540.1 billion by the end of FY 1995, of which the CSRS component accounted for $538.3 billion (US GAO 1996). To place this large sum in perspective, it is more than 10 times the size of the assets in the Thrift Savings Plan and nearly half the size of all private sector defined benefit plan assets in the United States.

This unfunded liability represents that portion of estimated future benefit obligations that has gone unrecognized by the government, in the sense that they are not backed by special issue Treasury securities. To the extent that it is merely an actuarial estimate, whether plan obligations are funded or unfunded has no effect on current budget outlays. Moreover, the degree of unfunding is not a measure of the government's ability to pay plan retirement benefits in the future. A primary result of not fully funding government pension plans is that agencies' budgets have not included the full cost of pensions.

Federal Borrowing. The Thrift Savings Plan assets played a role in the budget battle between President Clinton and Congress. In 1995, the Secretary of the Treasury suspended issuance of Government debt to the G fund of the Thrift Savings Plan. The suspension lasted from November 15, 1995 to March 29, 1996, when legislation was passed to increase the federal debt limit. The Secretary did this after Congress refused to raise the federal debt ceiling, which threatened to throw the government into default on its debt payments. The government has since repaid the amount of principal and interest into the G fund that would have been in that fund had there been no suspension. In the interim, the funds that would have been invested in government securities were recorded on the books of the Thrift Savings Plan as funds on deposit at the Treasury. At the end of 1995, that account equaled $9 billion.

The suspension took many people by surprise, as most pension and budgetary experts did not realize that the Secretary of the Treasury had that authority. Many experts have considered that an improper use of retirement funds of federal government workers.

Benefit Generosity. Because nearly all workers who had the option to choose between the old and new systems choose to remain in the old system, it can be inferred that most workers felt that the old system was more generous. Because the two systems differ in a number of respects, it is not possible to compare precisely the relative generosity of the two systems.

In the new system, the Thrift Savings Plan is an important part of the benefits of retirees. For workers who invested the maximum amount of 15 percent of salary in the Thrift Savings Plan and invested it all in the stock fund, the benefits provided by the new system are considerably more generous than for workers who invested the minimum amount of one percent of pay and invested it entirely in the government bond fund. Because of the strength of the US stock market in recent years, workers who have invested the maximum amount in the stock market may receive considerably more generous benefits than similarly situated workers participating in the old system. Studies have shown that higher paid workers and men were more likely to contribute the maximum amount to the Thrift Savings Plan and to invest entirely in the stock fund (Hinz, McCarthy, and Turner 1996).

Conclusions

The reform of the U.S. civil service pension system achieved the following objectives:

It brought newly hired civil servants into the social security system, which improved the financial outlook of that system and moved social security closer to universal coverage.

It resulted in a retirement system for federal government workers more comparable to that of private sector workers. In that context, the reform made the system appear more equitable, since the system it replaced seemed to be overly generous in some of its provisions.

It raised the minimum retirement age by two years, bringing the minimum retirement age more in line with that prevailing in private sector pension plans.

It partially privatized federal government retirement by instituting a funded defined contribution plan with some private sector investment. This was done by providing a 401(k)-type of plan to federal workers. These plans have been very popular in the private sector.

It improved portability for federal government employees, facilitating mobility into and out of the civil service.

Notes

1. The information reported in this section is taken from Federal Retirement Thrift Investment Board (1991, p. B-69), which reports a descriptive analysis of these data. Most employees who began working for the federal government before January 1, 1984 are covered by the Civil Service Retirement System. Generally, employees who began working for the federal government after 1983 are covered by FERS.

2. Much of the remainder of this section draws on the discussion of pp. 14-15 in US GAO 1995.

References

Arthur Andersen. "Report of Independent Public Accountants." Washington, DC, March 12, 1997

Federal Retirement Thrift Investment Board. "Annual Report", 1991

Hinz, Richard, David McCarthy and John Turner. "Are Women Conservative Investors? Gender Differences in Participant Directed Pension Investments." In *Positioning Pensions for the Year 2000*, Olivia Mitchell (ed.). Philadelphia: University of Pennsylvania Press, 1996.

Ippolito, Richard A. "Why Federal Workers Don't Quit," *The Journal of Human Resources* XXII 2: 281-299, 1987.

Social Security Administration. "A Pension From Work Not Covered By Social Security." Publication No. 05-10045. January, 1996.

U.S. General Accounting Office (GAO). "Overview of Federal Retirement Programs." May 22. Testimony of Johnny C. Finch, Assistant Comptroller General, General Government Programs before the Subcommittee on Post Office and Civil Service Committee on Governmental Affairs of the U.S. Senate (Report No. GAO/T-GGD-95-172), 1995.

U.S. General Accounting Office (GAO). "Public Pensions: Summary of Federal Pension Plan Data." February. Report No. GAO-AIMD-96-6, 1996.

U.S. General Accounting Office (GAO). "Federal Retirement: Federal and Private Sector Retirement Program Benefits Vary." April. (Report No. GGD-97-40), 1997

U.S. Office of Personnel Management. *1995 Federal Personnel Guide*. Washington: GPO, 1995.

Part II THE STATE AS PENSION REGULATOR

8 REGULATION OF PENSIONS IN THE UK

Sue Ward

Introduction

This paper deals mainly with *occupational* pensions. These are pensions provided by the employer, on which the UK relies very heavily. Most of the problems of regulation arise with private sector employers, rather than those in the public services, although the framework of U.K. pensions law does not make the clear-cut distinctions there are in some other countries.

Background

Occupational pension provision has existed for more than two centuries in the UK, with the first recognisable private sector scheme dating back to 1770, for the East India Company's staff. There was a large growth of provision with the railway companies in the nineteenth century, with many of the schemes being established by private Act of Parliament. It is worth pointing out, because it has been a continuing thread running through issues of regulation of pensions, and especially requirements on how those who leave the employer are to be treated, that from the first, schemes were coercive as well as benevolent. The benefits were a reward for employees' loyalty, and could be forfeited, even the day before retirement was due, for taking strike action or other "misconduct" as defined by the employer.

The Inland Revenue (tax authorities) started taking an interest in the 1920s, and granted certain tax advantages to "approved" schemes. The rules for approval have changed many times over this century, but for most of that time they have been the most potent force in the regulation of occupational pensions. The Revenue's interest, like that of all tax authorities, is not in the welfare of scheme members, but in stopping tax avoidance, so their approval rules concentrate on the *maximum* amounts of benefits that may be provided, and the maximum levels of funds that can be built up.

A specialist office of the Inland Revenue, the Pension Schemes Office, imposes these controls, mainly through a series of published "Practice Notes" and – only in the last few years – a programme of "compliance audits". There is nothing to stop an employer running an "unapproved" scheme. Since there is a ceiling on the level of pay that can be treated as *pensionable* in an approved scheme, this is often done for highly paid employees, but they do not receive the same tax advantages.

The Inland Revenue takes an interest mainly when a scheme is being set up, or when the rules are being amended, though there are some areas where they need to give specific approval before the scheme can take action. They are not concerned with how well or badly schemes are run, so long as they comply.

Alongside the Inland Revenue sit the Social Security authorities, who are concerned mainly with schemes that have "contracted out" of the State Earnings Related Scheme (SERPS), under our peculiar British system. Until April 1997, supervision of contracting-out lay with the Occupational Pensions Board (OPB) within the DSS. They had to certify that schemes met the requirements. But there has been *de*regulation here, with the requirement to provide a guaranteed level of benefits in a contracted out scheme being first of all modified in 1988 and then dropped altogether for 1997 onwards, and placing the responsibility for certifying that schemes meet the new standards on the scheme's professional advisers, not the Department. It is too early to say how these arrangements will work in the longer term.

A further body, set up in 1991, is the Registry of Occupational and Personal Pension Schemes. This was left over from a previous failed attempt at regulation. Under the 1985 Social Security Act – brought in as a result of one of the many reports calling for reform of the regulatory system in the 1980s – the Government set up a Registrar to whom all Annual Reports and Accounts of pension schemes were to be sent. It would have been open to individuals to look at these, as they can with company accounts. But there were protests mainly from employers, that corporate "asset strippers" would go and look at the Register and find schemes with large surpluses in their funds and then bid for the companies. So this part of the legislation was never brought into force, and it was abolished in 1990. Instead, a later Register was set up as simply a tracing service, holding names and addresses of schemes, so that people who had lost touch with their employers could find out where to claim their pension from.

The fourth element in the framework of regulation is trust law. Many of the early schemes were set up under private Act of Parliament, but where this was not done, it was apparent that there needed to be a legal device to safeguard the pensions in the event of the employer disappearing. The device that was used – and that word is appropriate, because it was often not much more than a legal fiction – was the "trust" under English common law. This is a very old form of legal structure, developed primarily to deal with the holding of family property. The example that is always given in the textbooks and lectures is that of the knight going off on crusade, leaving his castle in the care of his best friend, and then coming back and finding the friend had taken over and pulled the drawbridge up against him. Instead of starting a new war about it, trust law enabled him to go to court and invoke the King's power to enforce his ownership.

Other countries, with a Roman law framework, have evolved rather different answers to the problem of how to separate the pension arrangements from the employer's day to day business. In the UK, trust law was used but not adapted. It fits unhappily with the fact that pensions are deferred pay earned through one's employment, and it is also extremely expensive for the individual to enforce any rights under trust law. Since 1991 there has been a Pensions Ombudsman, who is in effect a one-man judicial tribunal ruling on whether trustees have been guilty of breaches of trust law or maladministration. The first Pensions Ombudsman did not make a great deal of impact, but the second one has been making some decisions that are very controversial with employers. Though the bulk of his work is redressing the grievances of individuals, in a number of high-profile cases he has looked at decisions of trustees on the scheme as a whole, in particular on the use of surplus funds.

Overlaid on all these was a patchwork of statutory requirements, for instance on equal access to schemes for men and women, or information to be provided to members, incorporated in various Acts of Parliament. Some of these included enforcement arrangements; a number of the more recent ones, especially on information-giving and investing the scheme's funds in the employer's business, have not.

Critique of Regulatory Framework

The Goode Committee, (discussed below), made strong criticisms of the framework of law and regulation when it reported in 1993. To quote selectively from the key chapter (HMSO, 1993):

"Fundamentally, it lacks structure and organisation and does not adequately resolve conflicting policy objectives. It allows such wide powers and discretions to be conferred on the employer and the trustees in the scheme documents that the interests of scheme members are not always sufficiently protected. The current statutory framework does not provide a position of neutrality. A number of requirements and restrictions which in principle ought to be applied across the board cover earnings-related schemes but not money-purchase schemes, or self-administered schemes but not insured schemes. The existing disputes resolution procedure is inadequate. The law is complex and in many respects uncertain. Further, the limited scope of the solvency requirements, coupled with the absence of any proper scheme of compensation for members where the employer becomes insolvent, means that scheme members can suffer great hardship. Finally, there is no regulatory body with overall jurisdiction over occupational pension schemes and equipped with the range of powers needed to monitor and enforce proper standards of pension scheme administration." (par. 4.1.2)

"The root of the problem is that there is no comprehensive legal framework governing occupational pensions.... Pensions law is an amalgam of equity and trust law, contract and labour law, heavily overlaid with complex legislation governing the occupational pensions aspects of social security, taxation and financial services. One can search in vain for a code in which the essential rights and obligations flowing from the establishment of pension schemes are clearly laid out. Much of the law is to be found only in reports of court decisions about the interpretation of scheme documents and the duties of trustees and employers at common law. Legislation is at present spread over more than thirty statues and well over a hundred statutory instruments. The planned consolidation Act for occupational pensions.... will do nothing to resolve the much greater problem of complex subordinate legislation, not to mention the profusion of memoranda, guidance notes, practice notes and other documents produced by the various Government departments and professional bodies. Nor will it deal with the fundamental weakness of the present system, the lack of a properly structured framework of rights and obligations. (par. 4.1.6)

"Several consequences flow from the lack of a more clearly defined and accessible set of legal rules governing pension schemes. First, there is great uncertainty both as to the content and as to the source of their rights and obligations of parties to pension schemes.... Second, because of the vacuum in the general law relating to pension schemes, tax legislation and Inland Revenue discretionary powers have been used to bring in matters of pension policy and not merely of fiscal policy. Thus the conditions of approval of schemes for the purpose of tax relief are made the vehicle for rules about funding and the segregation of assets, and restrictions on alienation of pensions, which should form part of the general law.... Thirdly, there is in certain respects a confusion of policy objectives. It is inevitable that there should be tension between the concern of the DSS to maximise pension provision and that of the Inland Revenue to avoid excessive loss of revenue, but some of the Inland Revenue rules would seem unintentionally to militate against prudent scheme management." (par. 4.1.7)

Maxwell and the Goode Committee

That was the situation in 1991 when Mr Robert Maxwell disappeared from his yacht in the Atlantic. In a sense, the robbery of his employees' pension fund that was then revealed was a disaster waiting to happen. If there was an assumption behind the framework of pension regulation, it was that schemes were run by people of goodwill with the members' interests at heart. This left it wide open to people who were not of goodwill. There had been pension scheme scandals before. There are still cases outstanding from the Hill Kestrel scandal ten years ago, for example, where a couple of people set up phoney pension schemes, persuaded others to transfer their money into them, and then disappeared. But there has been nothing on the Maxwell scale, and nothing that caught the media limelight. Post Maxwell, things had to change, but the question was the extent of change.

So the Conservative Government set up the Goode Committee, of which I was a member. The committee put forward a package of proposals for reform, which were intended to be taken as a package. The proposals have been criticised, but they would have created a fair and workable set of arrangements.

There is a *fundamental* problem with regulation, when something is voluntary for employers to provide, and where they are not going to make a profit – in fact, they are going to incur a cost – when they do. Why should they bother? In that situation, if you impose rules the employer considers burdensome – even if in fact they are plain commonsense or good management – some at least of them will find other ways of doing the same thing, or give up doing it altogether. This problem is exacerbated by the employment atmosphere in the UK over the last two decades, where there is not the same social pressure to seek a consensus and common interest between employers and employees as in other parts of Europe.

The Goode Committee made a series of recommendations, proposing that trust law should be retained as the framework but there should be changes in the management of schemes, the role of trustees, financial solvency requirements, rules on internal disputes, among others. The report also proposed the setting up of a new regulator for occupational pension schemes. It said (HMSO, 1993) that:

> "A major weakness of the present law governing occupational pension schemes is that there is no statutory authority with overall responsibility for their supervision and for enforcement of the legal responsibilities governing them...The new legal framework we have recommended depends for its effectiveness on proper supervisory and enforcement machinery. We therefore recommend that the Pensions Regulator should have wide-ranging functions and powers." (par. 4.19.22)

> "The tasks we have identified for the Regulator are substantial. If they are to be performed in the way we consider necessary for pension schemes to be properly safeguarded, it is important that the Regulator is organised in an effective way and that the resources necessary should be made available." (4.19.27)

The duties of the Regulator as proposed by the Goode Report included:

(a) registering schemes, such registration to be a prerequisite of Inland Revenue approval;

(b) monitoring schemes, and enforcing compliance with legal requirements, including rules relating to trustees, minimum solvency and disclosure;

(c) intervening in scheme administration where the scheme assets appear to the Regulator to be in jeopardy;

(d) receiving and investigating complaints of impropriety in the management of pension schemes or the composition or conduct of the trustees;

(e) disqualifying from acting in the management of an occupational pension scheme those who have shown themselves unfit to act and who are not automatically disqualified under Section 24 of this Part, and maintain a public register of those so disqualified;

(f) in defined circumstances, monitoring schemes that are being wound up or require them to be wound up; (par 4.19.23)

The Pensions Act bringing this in, the Report said, would:

> "provide a framework of general law that has hitherto been lacking; and it will also enable Inland Revenue rules to be confined to fiscal matters, with the incorporation of a general condition of tax approval that scheme rules must satisfy the provisions of the Act and any conditions imposed by the Pensions Regulator." (par. 4.1.7)

The 1995 Pensions Act

The 1995 Pensions Act followed the broad framework of the Goode Report, but with a number of important differences.

To summarise the biggest changes made by the Act are:

- Members of an occupational scheme are able to nominate a minimum of one-third of the trustees of that scheme, unless they have consented to an alternative package put forward by the employer.
- There is a Minimum Funding Requirement (MFR) for the funding of most final earnings pension schemes. The actuary must monitor this on behalf of the trustees at regular intervals. If the funding is falling short, the trustees must arrange with the employer to put things right. This is being phased in and will not be fully operational before the year 2007;
- There must be a written schedule of contributions. A record must also be kept of the date that contributions are made, or the action taken to recover the debt. Contributions deducted from employees' pay must be paid over to the scheme within 14 days after the end of the tax month. Unpaid contributions are a debt on the employer.
- Schemes must have a Statement of Investment Principles setting out how they intend to meet the MFR, their attitude to risk and diversification, how they will obtain advice and how they will monitor the investments.
- There are new requirements for record-keeping, the appointment of advisers and running of trustees' meetings, and the setting up of a disputes procedure.

The Act also included provision for a new regulatory body, the Occupational Pensions Regulatory Authority, OPRA. This is a much more limited body than that proposed by Goode. It is able to deal only with transgressions of particular statutory provisions under the Act and the main Pension Schemes Act 1993. Though it can remove trustees if it decides they are unfit for the job, and replace them with others, it does *not* have a general supervisory role over the behaviour of trustees outside their statutory duties. Breach of trust is left to "private law" enforcement, that is by individuals taking the trustees to court, or going to the Ombudsman.

Certain sections of the Act, covering indexation of pensions, and equal treatment, are specifically excluded from OPRA's ambit. The last Government said (House of Lords, 1995a) that these matters could be left to the Ombudsman or Industrial Tribunals, though if widespread misbehaviour by a particular scheme occurred, there probably would be maladministration which might come to OPRA's attention in other spheres. The Inland Revenue's role remains unchanged, while the DSS's supervision over contracting out has been altered in the way described above. The Pensions Ombudsman's powers have been somewhat widened, in particular to deal with disputes between groups of trustees.

As a result of this, there is still fragmented regulation. There might be a danger of turf wars, but it does not seem to be happening. Under Sections 107 and 108 of the Act, OPRA is empowered to disclose information obtained to a long list of other parties, mainly regulators, for the purpose of helping them fulfil their duties. OPRA is also able to seek information from other parties. That comes partly under the compulsory powers in section 98, partly through the legal gateways such as section 109 of the Act, and partly through Memoranda of Understanding with other parties.

The first Memorandum was signed with OPAS (the Pensions Advisory Service), the Pensions Compensation Board, and the Pensions Ombudsman on 30 April 1997. Essentially the Ombudsman passes on material where he thinks OPRA should be starting an investigation, so that there is no need to go over the same ground twice. OPRA is discussing similar memoranda with the Contracted Out Employments Group of the DSS and with the Pension Schemes Office. There is every sign that no-one wants to see wrong-doing go undetected merely because the wrong body has valuable information which is not passed on to the correct investigator.

OPRA is a *reactive* regulator. Instead of asking for standardised compliance reporting and monitoring visits, people are required to report their own, or their clients' *non*-compliance.

This is not what the Goode Report originally proposed. It said (HMSO, 1993) that:

> "An important element in the monitoring structure is the duty that would be laid on trustees to file reports and accounts with the Regulator. Delay in filing documents is often one of the best indicators that all is not well with the organisation concerned. The Regulator will also be alerted to possible difficulties where the reports of the scheme auditor or the scheme actuary are qualified." (par 4.19.26)

The Government's argument for rejecting this was that "it is neither practical nor desirable for the authority to supervise and regularly monitor over 150,000 pension schemes, most of which are perfectly well-run" (House of Lords, 1995b).

So Section 48 of the Act reads:

> "If the auditor or actuary of any occupational pension scheme has reasonable cause to believe that -
> (a) any duty relevant to the administration of the scheme imposed by any enactment or rule of law on the trustees or managers, the employer, any professional adviser or any prescribed person acting in connection with the scheme has not been or is not being complied with, and
> (b) the failure to comply is likely to be of material significance in the exercise by the Authority of any of their functions,
> he must immediately give a written report of the matter to the Authority."

This has been fleshed out by guidance from OPRA itself, and from the actuarial and accountancy professional bodies.

OPRA has the powers to do some routine compliance monitoring, writing to a sample of schemes, or visiting them, and asking them for evidence that they comply, and it is doing this, but the resources are not geared to doing a great deal of it. The small scale monitoring is intended to protect it against two possible dangers for a regulator; one would be that it might get a jaundiced view of the industry, seeing only the villains because it never had anything to do with the virtuous. The other is that it might have too rosy a view – that if it were seen as ineffectual, no-one might complain so that it concluded that there were no villains either.

OPRA only took up its functions in April 1997, and the statistics to end-June 1997 were that around 3,000 case files had been created. Only a tiny proportion of them were cases that were being investigated for fraud. The vast majority were concerns about administration, about whether trustees were pursuing their duties in the right way, or about using the new law to rectify past difficulties. For example, it is now a *criminal* offence by the employer not to have paid over employees' contributions to the scheme by the 19th of the month following their deduction from the employees' pay, without reasonable excuse. Many smaller employers seem to be having difficulty in meeting this deadline, and so many of the reports that have come in concern this late payment.

To give another example, there are hundreds of schemes without trustees. One insurer has reported 700 of these, another 300. The problem arises because of the common and never very sensible practice of drafting trust deeds for smaller schemes so that the employer acts as the sole corporate trustee. Then the employer disappears, and since it is an insured money purchase scheme the insolvency practitioner has no duty to appoint an independent trustee – so stalemate. That leaves a vacuum in the trusteeship, which can mean the members are unable to get access to the funds for transfers or even their retirement.

There was nothing that could be done about this in the past, but now OPRA is able to appoint trustees to schemes where there is a need, and this may well be the most common action we are called upon to perform in our first 12 months.

OPRA has the power to impose swingeing penalties, including fines and disqualifications, and in some circumstances to recommend criminal prosecution in the Courts, but it has the discretion to decide whether or not to impose those penalties. There are also "firefighting" powers to enable it to protect the interests of scheme members and to help safeguard scheme assets, including powers to take out injunctions restraining individuals from certain actions, and to recover misappropriated assets. So far, it has not done any of these things, though the time is not that far off when it will be considering it

Pensions Industry's Response

Although OPRA is nothing like the regulator proposed by Goode, it is still a step change for those running pension schemes. Their duties have been tightened up and codified, and more important there are potential penalties for not doing things, or not doing them quickly enough, where there were none before. Though there were fears before the Act came into force, in general the pensions industry has responded reasonably well to the change. But there has been some misunderstanding of OPRA's role, with requests from people to "waive" the legal requirements, although OPRA does not have the power to do this, because it is a statutory body enforcing statute law. The confusion arises partly because the regulators in financial services are "self-regulatory organisations" who make their own rules, and so can waive or change those rules.

There is some discretion on what sanctions or penalties are imposed for non-compliance with the law, and OPRA is also able to give guidance on the form of reports expected. On certain aspects of the Act OPRA does not have direct enforcement powers, such as indexation or equal treatment. The guidance is that there is no need to report breaches solely in those areas, nor about breaches before 7 April 1997 which have been put right or where there is nothing OPRA can do about them anyway – such as earlier failures to produce scheme accounts. But reports are required about breaches of general law and trust law, of a type that might cast doubt on trustees' fitness to continue in office, even though they may not have breached the Act itself. And clearly, any breaches coming to the attention of the scheme actuary or auditor which indicate potential dishonesty or the misuse of assets or contributions, or which carry criminal sanctions, ought *always* to be reported.

For practical reasons, OPRA took during its first year a slightly different approach in two areas. One is where a scheme is being wound up. This is not a simple matter, and can take a very long time. The statutory requirements include winding-up schemes as much as any other, but there is no point – and often no money – to implement some of these. OPRA does not have the power to waive reporting requirements, but has requested a very brief report from the professionals saying where the gaps are, and when they hope to complete the winding up of the scheme. There have been a great many such reports – pages and pages of them from one source, in some cases.

It is not possible for OPRA to fetter its discretion in individual cases, but it has said that it will not impose sanctions for every failure to implement procedures laid down under the Act, while the scheme is being wound up. It regards the members' interests as paramount and expect trustees and advisers to act accordingly.

The other practical issue was on transitional breaches. OPRA's board knew, just as well as the rest of the pensions industry, that some of the regulations and professional guidance were issued very late, and that there were schemes which did not manage to tie up all their loose ends before 6 April 1997. So it was announced for these schemes that it was acceptable to send in a very short report, indicating the nature of the breach and the dates by which the matter is to be remedied. But OPRA expected this will not be longer than 3 months – so 6th July 1997 at latest. The staff now follow up such reports carefully. If someone has said they are having a trustee meeting to finalise things on 30 June, for instance, there is a requirement to contact them afterwards to check that they did so.

The Board had to give some additional leeway for the time taken on calculation of the amount of money to be transferred between pension schemes, or to a Personal Pension, when someone moved, because the Chancellor caused some chaos (and a lot of opposition) in the pensions industry in his first Budget, by changing the taxation arrangements for pension scheme investments.

The actuaries and auditors play a crucial role. The Act includes powers for OPRA to impose penalties on those who do not comply with the whistleblowing duties, but they have not yet been brought into force. The last Government said that it would rely on the professional bodies to discipline their members, but it is not yet clear how that will work in practice.

Conclusions

This section does not provide a critique of the new regulatory arrangements, partly because it would not be appropriate, but also because it is too early. OPRA has been open for business for less than 15 months and several parts of the Act have yet to bite. With member-nominated trustees, arrangements did not have to be in place until October 1997, or even April 1998 in some cases. The new requirements on scheme annual reports only apply for scheme years ending after 6 April 1997, while existing scheme members need have new information disclosed to them only within a year of the Act's coming into force. And on the Minimum Funding Requirement for scheme solvency the ultimate compliance date is as far off as April 2007. We are also in the middle of an economic upturn. The point when pension schemes are most vulnerable is during a recession, when employers are feeling short of money. There will have to be a full economic cycle before we can judge how effective the new arrangements really are.

Instead this section offers some *personal* thoughts about some of the principles of regulation for pensions. The Labour Government is currently undertaking a full review of pensions policy (yet another one). Among the "fundamental challenges" they want to deal with (see Department of Social Security, 1997) are:

> "To ensure resources devoted to pensions are used as efficiently and effectively as possible, whether this comes directly from individuals and employers, or indirectly from them through the tax system; and
>
> "To get the regulation of pensions right, finding a balance which provides an appropriate level of security, minimises the scope for abuse, and does not impose an undue burden on providers;"

If they wish to achieve this, they should bear in mind the following points:

- First, to reiterate a point made earlier, there is a *fundamental* problem with how firm you can make your regulation, when something is voluntary for employers to provide, and where they are not going to make a profit when they do. There is considerable pressure on the Government to compel people to provide far more for their pensions – rather than just the limited alternatives of a low SERPS benefit or contracted-out arrangements which can be minimal. If there is compulsion of this sort, the whole atmosphere changes. The regulation of both those who are being compelled, and of those who are taking on the business, changes. Government can be quite heavy-handed with the employers or employees or both, depending on exactly what is compulsory – is it the Swiss situation where the employers must pay into pensions for their employees, or the Chilean one where employees are entirely responsible for buying their own pensions? But if people *must* pay into a fund run by a private body, those providers hold considerable power. Regulators can say to them, "you must offer minimum standards, if you want the business," but there may well come a point where they say, "on the terms you are demanding, we don't want the business." It becomes a matter of negotiation as much as regulation.

- Secondly, the framework changes as soon as choice is provided. If the regulatory burdens vary between different options, then employers and providers at least will look for the lightest regulator – though the employees might think rather differently. In the UK, there is the option for the employer to organise a bulk-purchase of personal (individual) pensions for the employees, rather than sponsor an occupational pension scheme. There are big differences in the regulatory framework of these Group Personal Pensions, which are proving quite attractive to some.

    An example of this is the position on employers paying over contributions to schemes. With an occupational scheme, as explained earlier, there are now very tight requirements. But where the employer is sponsoring a Group Personal Pension scheme, making the deductions from the employees' pay and possibly adding something herself, the rules are much less clear. The insurance companies are supposed to notify the members about any shortfall, but often do not.

- Finally, once individuals are offered a choice, marketing costs go up – and so the amount being used constructively in the pension goes down – and the need for regulation goes up. The Australians are moving from a situation where the pension fund employees pay into depends on the industrial agreement covering them, to one where the employer must offer at least 5 different funds to employees. The Australian trade unions have advertised in national newspapers, warning they will take action against providers who act irresponsibly, having learnt the lessons of the British experience of "mis-selling". One major problem, if that goes through, is that those who are doing the buying, and those who are bearing the cost of any mistakes, are different. The providers will be making their sales pitches at the employers, to put them on their "preferred" list, but if something goes wrong, it's the ordinary member who bears the cost.

Life is much simpler when pension provision is made through the State or national institutions, unfashionable though it may be to say so!

References

Department of Social Security press release 97/122, 17 July 1997

House of Lords, *Hansard*, 7 February 1995a, col. 157 (Lord Lucas)

House of Lords, *Hansard*, 7 February 1995b, col. 109 (Lord Mackay)

HMSO, *Pension Law Reform, Report of the Pension Law Review Committee*, (Goode Committee), CM 2342, London, HMSO, 1993.

9 SUPPLEMENTARY PENSIONS IN BRITAIN: IS THERE STILL A ROLE FOR THE STATE?

Tony Lynes

Introduction

On 5 March 1997, less than two months before losing power, the British Conservative Government gave its unequivocal answer to the question which is the title of this paper: a firm negative. Although entitled "Basic Pension Plus" (referred to below as BP+), the Government's plan for future pensions policy amounted to a proposal to abolish state pensions in Britain – both the flat-rate basic pension and the earnings-related supplementary pension (SERPS).

The Labour Party's statement of pensions policy, *Security in Retirement* published in June 1996, also envisaged a significant though less clearly defined shift of emphasis from state to private provision. At the party's annual conference in October 1996, serious concern was expressed about the direction in which the party appeared to be moving and, although the policy document was approved, it was agreed that a comprehensive review of pensions policy would be carried out after the expected change of Government. That change duly occurred in May 1997 and the policy review commenced in July. The original intention of publishing the Government's proposals in a 'green paper' in the first half of 1998 was not achieved and publication is now expected towards the end of 1998. A further, probably short, period of public consultation will follow before draft legislation is presented to Parliament.

The first section of this paper describes the Conservative BP+ proposals which, though unlikely to be implemented, are of interest as an attempt to carry the policy of privatisation of pensions to its logical conclusion. The second section summarises the Labour Party's policy position as set out in *Security in Retirement* and the party's manifesto for the May election. The third and main section discusses some of the options which might be considered in the policy review if the Government were not determined to reduce the role of the state in pension provision. The final section offers some tentative conclusions.

The Conservative plan: Basic Pension Plus

British state pensions comprise a flat-rate 'basic' pension (now £64.70 per week, about 16 per cent of the average earnings of adults in full-time employment) and an earnings-related supplementary pension (SERPS). The privatisation of supplementary pensions has already reached an advanced stage. The contracting-out arrangements introduced in 1978 and extended in 1987 allow employees to

75

contribute to occupational or personal pension schemes instead of SERPS, and two out of three employees are doing so. BP+ proposed to complete this process by closing SERPS to young people now beginning their working lives and requiring them to contribute 5% of their earnings to an occupational or personal scheme. (Department of Social Security, 1997a)

The contracting-out arrangements do not apply to the basic pension. The most controversial aspect of BP+ was the proposal to abolish the basic pension in its present form. In its place, part of the social security contributions paid by employees and employers (£9 per week per employee was suggested) was to be diverted from the state scheme and paid into a personal pension fund for each employee, operating on a 'money purchase' basis. Again, only those now entering the labour force and their successors would be affected, and they would not begin to reach pension age until about the year 2040.

An explicit proposal to abolish the basic pension – the sacred cow of the British social security system – even as far in the future as 2040 would have been extremely unpopular, especially as there could be no certainty that the money purchase pensions which were to replace it would be of equivalent value. The Government proposed, therefore, that the state should offer a guarantee: if the money-purchase replacement pension was less than the basic pension would have been, the state would pay the difference. This enabled the Government to claim that, far from abolishing the basic pension, it was guaranteeing its future value. As the minister, Peter Lilley, explained in a letter to Members of Parliament (Lilley, 1997): "The scheme is called the Basic Pension Plus because it builds on the present basic state pension. It is the basic pension – plus a personal fund, plus a state guarantee." A more accurate description would have been "a personal fund, plus a state guarantee – minus the basic pension."

An obvious objection to these proposals was the cost imposed on the new generation of workers, contributing to funded pension schemes for their own pensions while meeting the current cost of state pensions for those already retired. The Government proposed to reduce the effect on public finances by altering the tax treatment of occupational and personal pension schemes, but this would have meant simply that the transitional cost would be met through higher taxes on current earnings rather than through social security contributions.

A less obvious drawback, which the Government did its best to conceal, was the inadequacy of the resulting pensions. The minister claimed that, under BP+, a person with average earnings retiring around 2040 could expect a total pension of £175 per week (Lilley, 1997) – about 50% of average earnings in 1996. He was later forced to admit (House of Commons, 1997) that, on the basis of his own assumption that average earnings would rise each year by 2% more than prices, the £175 pension would be only 18.1% of average earnings for a man and 22.9% for a woman retiring in 2040 (assuming in both cases that the person concerned was in continuous employment throughout his or her working life – a particularly improbable assumption for a woman).

It may seem surprising that the Government's proposals involved replacing the basic pension with money-purchase personal pension schemes of the kind that had proved a major political embarrassment since their introduction in 1987 as a basis for contracting out of SERPS (large numbers of employees were wrongly advised to transfer to them from occupational pension schemes or SERPS, and the insurance companies and other responsible bodies are still engaged in the massive task of identifying and compensating them). The Government argued that, since the new schemes would be compulsory, there could be no risk of them being mis-sold. Compulsion, it was argued, would also reduce the cost of the schemes by eliminating the cost of selling them. (Department of Social Security, 1997) Neither argument, however, was wholly convincing. It could be argued with as much justification that compulsion would reduce the incentive to offer good value; and, while an insurance company would no longer have to persuade people to buy a personal pension scheme, it would still have to persuade them to buy from that company rather than from one of its competitors. However low the administrative costs might be, they would certainly be much higher than those of a pay-as-you-go basic pension administered by the Department of Social Security.

The Labour plan: *Security in Retirement*

The Labour Party's proposals (Labour Party, 1996) envisaged the preservation of both the basic state pension and SERPS, but with a major role for private (including money-purchase) schemes. The underlying aims were set out as follows:

"Our strategy must therefore:

- establish the right balance between the state and the individual in providing for retirement
- ensure that everyone who is able to do so makes a responsible commitment to their own retirement income
- give appropriate support to those who cannot be expected to provide entirely for their retirement from their own income
- assist those who are already retired yet face a retirement in poverty or on declining incomes
- promote public understanding of pensions so that people can plan for the future and so that Governments today and in the future cannot shirk their responsibilities.
  We have one over-arching objective: to ensure that all pensioners, today and tomorrow, share fairly in the increasing prosperity of the nation."

The document pointedly avoided any commitment to reverse the changes in state pensions, both basic and SERPS, made by Conservative Governments since 1980. Regarding the basic pension, in one of its least inspiring sentences, the document proclaimed:

"The basic state pension is currently indexed to prices and Labour would not reduce this commitment ..."

The absence of any promise to restore the link with average earnings, broken in 1980, was underlined by the emphasis placed on plans to help the poorest pensioners by ensuring that they receive the minimum income to which they are entitled subject to a means test.

The brief references to SERPS showed a remarkable lack of enthusiasm for a scheme which, on its introduction, had been regarded as one of the major achievements of the last Labour Government:

"... SERPS could not easily or sustainably be rebuilt in its original form. New
      funded pension schemes could produce better returns for the same
      contribution level for many people.
But we also want to retain maximum choice for individuals ... We will
      therefore retain SERPS as an option for those who prefer to remain in it."

In one respect, Security in Retirement did propose an expansion of the role of
SERPS. It suggested that a "citizenship pension" could be provided for people who
could not reasonably be expected to obtain an adequate "second pension" through
their own savings, by "crediting them into SERPS". Two "obvious examples" were
given: low-paid workers and "carers" (those caring for other people without
financial reward). For those in paid employment but without access to occupational
pension schemes, however, new private funded schemes were proposed as the main
source of second pensions. These money-purchase "stakeholder" schemes would
generally be large: unlike most existing occupational schemes they would not be
limited to the employees of one firm but would be "multi-employer", enabling them
to operate more efficiently and more cheaply than personal pension schemes.
SERPS, it was implied, would remain only as a last resort for those unable to make
satisfactory arrangements in the private sector.

These proposals were summarised briefly in the Labour Party's manifesto for
the May 1 general election, the contents of which are morally binding on the new
Government. Again it was asserted that "all pensioners should share fairly in the
increasing prosperity of the nation". The basic pension would be increased "at least
in line with prices", which theoretically left open the possibility of the earnings link
being restored. The stakeholder pensions proposal, the commitment to retain SERPS
and the idea of a "citizenship pension" based on it were repeated and the intention of
setting up a review of pensions policy was confirmed. (Labour Party, 1997).

The Review

The review of pensions policy by officials of the Department of Social Security
headed by a minister, John Denham, was formally announced on 17 July 1997, $2^{1}/_{2}$
months after the Labour election victory. A large number of organisations and
individuals were invited to submit comments. Its terms of reference were:

"To review the central areas of insecurity for elderly people including all aspects
of the basic pension and its value and second pensions including SERPS; to
build a sustainable consensus for the long term future of pensions; and to publish
the Government's proposals, for further consultation, in the first part of 1998."
(Department of Social Security, 1997b)

(i)   The Basic Pension

In relation to the basic pension, the main issue is simple: will the link between the
pension and average earnings be restored? The case for restoring it is undeniably
strong. For most of the present generation of pensioners, especially those aged 75 or
over, the basic pension represents a large proportion of their total income, and it is
difficult to see any other way of fulfilling the promise that they will share fairly in
the increasing prosperity of the nation over the remaining years of their lives.

Improvements in means-tested benefits and measures to encourage people to claim those benefits would help only the minority who are entitled to them. Occupational pensions, once in payment, are at best indexed to prices and do not reflect rising living standards. Other ways of raising the real incomes of pensioners, such as the lump-sum payments made this year as a contribution to their winter fuel bills, are unlikely to provide more than a small fraction of what would be needed to maintain even the present relationship between pensioners' and employees' incomes. Indeed, one of the attractions of such payments, for a Government committed to rigorous control of public expenditure, is that they give the impression of generosity while reducing the pressure for pension increases which would be much more costly.

For future generations of pensioners, the value of the basic pension may become less important as the proportion receiving earnings-related second pensions increases, but there will be large numbers of low-paid and intermittent workers (mainly women) with little or no entitlement to earnings-related pensions. There is also an egalitarian argument for maintaining the value of the basic pension relative to earnings: it provides a redistributive element, preventing the inequalities of earnings from being fully reflected in retirement income.

The main national organisation representing pensioners, the National Pensioners Convention (NPC), in its submissions to the pensions review (National Pensioners Convention, 1998), in the drafting of which the present writer played a major part, demanded not only the restoration of the link between the basic pension and average earnings but the gradual recovery, over a five-year period, of the ground already lost through the breaking of the link in 1980 (about £22 per week or one-third of the present value of the pension). The first pension increase under the new Government, however, in April 1998, was based on the increase in prices, following the previous Government's practice, and there is little expectation that the earnings link will be restored for future years, while action to restore past losses is even less likely. A more probable outcome of the review would be an undertaking, without any legal requirement, to consider from year to year whether and to what extent increases in the basic pension should reflect "rising national prosperity".

(ii) The State Earnings-Related Pension (SERPS)

SERPS in its original form, as introduced in 1978, was intended to provide a pension of 25 per cent of the earnings on which contributions were payable, and the accrual rate was to be increased in the early years so that anyone more than 20 years below pension age when the scheme commenced in 1978 would, if continuously employed, be entitled to the 25 per cent pension. For most of those contributing to the scheme for more than 20 years, the pension would still have been only 25 per cent of earnings but its value would have been considerably enhanced by the fact that only their 20 best years of earnings were to be used in the pension calculation. In 1986, however, the law was changed: the pension rate was to be reduced for those reaching pension age in the 21st century, from 25 to 20 per cent, and the pension was to be based on lifetime earnings instead of the 20 best years. The prospective value of SERPS pensions was roughly halved by these changes.

The value of SERPS has also been affected indirectly by the breaking of the link between the basic pension and average earnings. The band of earnings which forms the contribution base in any year is determined by the current value of the basic pension: the lower earnings limit for contributions is approximately equal to the basic pension[1] and the upper limit is about 7 times that amount. The fall in the value of the basic pension, relative to average earnings, since 1980 has therefore lowered the band of earnings to which SERPS applies.

The short-term effect is mixed. Employees whose earnings are below the upper limit now pay contributions (and acquire pension rights) on a larger proportion of their total earnings. Those with earnings substantially above the upper limit, on the other hand, pay contributions on a smaller proportion of their earnings and their pension rights are correspondingly reduced. Commenting on the longer-term effects of the fall in the upper earnings limit as a proportion of average earnings (Lynes, 1996, p. 4), I wrote:

> "The long-term effect, if this process continues, will be catastrophic. The Government Actuary has estimated that if earnings rise by 1½ per cent more than prices each year, the upper earnings limit will have fallen to two-thirds of male average earnings by about 2030 (House of Commons, 1995, p. 8). Eventually, nearly everyone will have earnings above the upper limit and the pension will virtually cease to be earnings-related and become merely a small flat-rate addition to the basic pension."

In the light of these facts, it is not enough to say that SERPS "could not easily or sustainably be rebuilt in its original form". Without a change of policy, SERPS will not even survive in its present reduced form. If it is to have any useful long-term role, other than that of providing citizenship pensions for non-earners, it seems essential that the upper earnings limit should again be linked to average earnings.

But should SERPS have a long-term role? The Government's openly expressed preference is that, for employees not covered by occupational pension schemes, second pensions should as far as possible be provided by the proposed new breed of private money-purchase stakeholder pension schemes, not by SERPS. That preference is shared by the insurance companies and other commercial interests involved in the provision of private pension schemes. As a result, public discussion of the issues has been extremely one-sided. A 'consultation document' on stakeholder pension schemes (Department of Social Security, 1997) was published in November 1997, inviting views on how the schemes should operate and summarily dismissing the SERPS alternative:

> "To use SERPS as the basis for a significant expansion and improvement in second pensions ... would raise some difficult issues. Its pay-as-you-go nature, in particular, would place the main burden of any increase in pensions on future generations."

The task of defending SERPS and discussing the ways in which it could best contribute to the overall pattern of pension provision has been undertaken mainly by the NPC. In a submission to the pensions review, it noted the following advantages of SERPS over other second pension schemes:

- As a defined benefit scheme, SERPS provides pensions of a predictable proportion of earnings.

- The SERPS pension formula, based on the individual's earnings throughout his or her career, is much fairer than the 'final salary' formula used in most occupational schemes which favours white-collar workers, especially those receiving large salary increases shortly before retirement.
- SERPS provides pension rights which are fully portable, unlike occupational schemes, even the best of which penalise members who leave before pension age.
- SERPS can protect the pension rights of those temporarily excluded from paid employment.

In addition, in response to the stakeholder pensions consultation document, the NPC noted that the proposals put forward by a number of insurance companies implied a level of charges for administration which would absorb about one-quarter of the contributions paid by a person contributing to the scheme throughout his or her working life. The corresponding expense ratio for state pensions, including SERPS, is little more than 1 per cent. (National Pensioners Convention, 1998).

Whatever advantages SERPS may have, however, adequacy is not one of them. As noted above, this is in part due to the changes made by the 1986 Social Security Act – but only in part. Even in its original form, the scheme was designed to produce pensions of only about 25 per cent of relevant earnings, increased to a varying and unpredictable extent by the "20 best years" provision. For those reaching pension age in the first 20 years of the scheme (up to 1999), the accrual rate was doubled, giving them a very generous return on their contributions. Younger contributors were to receive a pension of the same proportion of earnings (originally 25 per cent of earnings, now reduced to 20 per cent) after 40 or more years of contributions. Yet a defined-benefit occupational scheme must provide, as a condition for contracting out of SERPS, a pension of 50 per cent of earnings after 40 years' contributions. To enable SERPS to provide a realistic alternative to schemes of this kind, the dramatic fall in the pension accrual rate for those retiring in the 21st century would have to be prevented. If that were done, the scheme would offer pensions of about 40 per cent of earnings within the contribution limits. Even then, with the contribution ceiling at its present level (£485 per week, about 1¼ times average earnings), SERPS would not meet the needs of higher-paid workers. If the earnings link had not been broken, the ceiling would now be about £650 per week (1¾ times average earnings). Raising it to that level would not seem unreasonable.

The case for restoring the "20 best years" formula is much less strong. It was intended to help those, mainly women, with interrupted careers or periods of abnormally low earnings, but it would have benefited, at great expense, nearly everyone with a contribution record extending over more than 20 years after 1978, the only exceptions being those whose earnings were above the ceiling in every single year. On the other hand, it offered nothing to those without any record of earnings above the lower earnings limit. It seems more rational to seek a solution along the lines of the 'citizenship pension' proposal, concentrating help on people in defined situations such as carers. It should be noted, however, that the term 'carers' can be interpreted narrowly to include only those caring for severely disabled people, or more broadly to include, in particular, the much larger number of women caring for young children. The present Government's policy in relation to the latter group is to encourage the provision of paid work rather than social security benefits, but there is a very strong case for protecting the pension rights of those who put the needs of their children first or cannot find jobs which are compatible with their parental role.

The changes suggested above would have major financial implications. In the long term, the value of SERPS pensions, and therefore their cost, would be more than doubled. Fewer people would be likely to contract out, increasing the cost still further. There would, however, be a corresponding increase in contribution income, which would come into effect immediately. This would arise not only from the increased number of SERPS contributors and the expansion of the contribution base, but also from the increase in contribution rates which would be a natural consequence of doubling the pension accrual rate.

At present, the whole of the state pension – both basic and SERPS – is financed on a pay-as-you-go basis. The very large short-term surpluses resulting from these changes would offer the possibility of building up a substantial fund over the next 20 years. There could be no question of making SERPS a fully funded scheme but partial funding would have a number of advantages. It would spread costs more fairly between the generations and help to compensate for the expected rise in the proportion of elderly people. It would ensure that the supposed economic benefits of pension funding were not lost in the event of an increase in the number of SERPS contributors. And it would help to restore public confidence in the state scheme, especially if the fund were seen to be administered by independent trustees.

The contracting-out terms would also have to be changed. The underlying principle is that the social security contributions of contracted-out employees are reduced by the amount that it would cost a private scheme to provide benefits similar to those of SERPS – the 'contracted-out rebate'. If SERPS benefits and the contributions going to finance them were to be increased, the contracted-out rebate would also have to be increased, so that contracted-out employees and their employers would continue to pay the same contributions to the state scheme.

The implications of this change would depend on whether the contracted-out scheme was a defined benefit or money-purchase scheme. In the case of a money-purchase scheme, the whole of the rebate must be paid into it. Increasing the rebate would reduce the scheme's expenses ratio, resulting in a more than proportionate increase in the pension. In view of the grossly inadequate pensions which the present rebate is expected to provide, this would be a desirable outcome.

Different considerations apply to contracted-out defined benefit schemes. They are already required to provide an adequate initial level of pension to employees whose membership continues up to pension age, at a cost which exceeds the present contracted-out rebate. Early leavers, however, generally lose part of their pension entitlement, and pensions in payment are not always fully protected from inflation. In return for the increased rebate, these schemes could be required to provide full preservation of early leavers' pensions and full inflation-proofing of pensions in payment.

Conclusion

Ideas of the kind outlined above are unlikely to find any place in the forthcoming green paper. The broad lines of Government policy are already clear. The role of the state, especially in the provision of second pensions, will continue to diminish and, in the short run, there will be little effective opposition to this trend. Few people understand the potential advantages of a defined-benefit state scheme over private money-purchase schemes, and the scandal surrounding the mis-selling of personal pensions has done little to erase the results of nearly two decades of anti-state pro-market propaganda. The main emphases of the green paper, therefore, are likely to be on the development of stakeholder schemes for those of working age and measures to promote take-up of income support and other means-tested benefits for those already in retirement. To provide adequately for both today's and tomorrow's pensioners, however, will require something more than a combination of private money-purchase schemes and public means-testing.

The role of the basic state pension remains crucial. It is the most important component of most pensioners' incomes and (in a commonly used metaphor) will "wither on the vine" if it continues to rise only in line with prices. The Government plainly does not intend to restore the earnings link as a statutory requirement, but it will take a good deal of ingenuity to fulfil the pledge of "fair shares in increasing prosperity for all pensioners" without regular increases in the real value of the basic pension.

The outlook for SERPS is more problematic. The Government is committed to keeping the scheme in existence for those who prefer it to the occupational and stakeholder alternatives, and past experience suggests that there is a substantial body of people with low earnings or on the margins of the labour market whose inclusion in private pension schemes of any kind is uneconomic. But if several million people are going to remain dependent on SERPS, measures will have to be taken to ensure the future viability of the scheme.

In the longer run, much may depend on how successful the new stakeholder pensions prove to be, but at best there will be a long transitional period during which very large numbers of pensioners will continue to rely mainly on the basic state pension, with or without the addition of income support. If their incomes fail to keep pace with the rise in the living standards of those in paid work - to say nothing of the living standards of pensioners in other European countries - a future Government may be compelled to restore the basic pension to at least its present level relative to average earnings. And if increasing numbers of SERPS contributors reach pension age with pensions below or only slightly above income support level, pressure may grow for a substantial improvement in the state's second pension scheme. In short, whatever the outcome of the current pensions review may be, the pensions debate will continue. That is the only certainty.

Notes

1. The Chancellor of the Exchequer announced on 17 March 1998 (House of Commons, 1998) that the lower earnings limit for contributions would be raised in April 1999 from £64 to £81 per week. It will, therefore, no longer be tied to the basic pension rate. Since no similar increase in the upper earnings limit is proposed, there will be a substantial reduction in total contributions, which the Chancellor described as "a tax cut for everyone in work". He stated that employees earning between £64 and £81 per week would "have their rights to benefit protected", but it is not clear whether this protection will extend to SERPS or will be limited to the basic pension and other flat-rate insurance benefits.

References

Department of Social Security. *New ambitions for our country: a new contract for welfare*, Cm 3805. London: The Stationery Office, 1998.

Department of Social Security. Press release 97/044. London: Department of Social Security, 1997a.

Department of Social Security. Press release 97/122. London: Department of Social Security, 1997b.

House of Commons. Parliamentary Debates, 11 March 1997. London: The Stationery Office, 1997.

House of Commons. Parliamentary Debates, 17 March 1998. London: The Stationery Office, 1998.

House of Commons, *National Insurance Fund Long Term Estimates*, HC 160, 1995.

Labour Party. *New Labour because Britain deserves better*. London: Labour Party, 1997.

Labour Party. *Road to the Manifesto: Security in Retirement*. London: Labour Party, 1996.

Lilley, P. Letter to Harriet Harman MP, 5 March 1997. London: Department of Social Security, 1997.

Lynes, T. *Our Pensions: a policy for a Labour Government*. London: Eunomia Publications, 1996.

National Pensioners Convention. *Pensions not Poor Relief*. London: National Pensioners Convention, 1998.

10

DUTCH GOVERNMENT PROPOSALS ON EARNINGS-RELATED PENSIONS AND MANDATORY PARTICIPATION

Erik Lutjens

Introduction

In September 1996 the Dutch Government presented proposals on the future of the social security system in the Netherlands. These proposals were laid down in a document titled 'Werken aan Zekerheid' (Building for Security). This document gives a description of the social security system in the Netherlands as a whole and in particular the position of occupational pensions within that system.

The central argument in the document is that social security is becoming too expensive, which makes cost restriction necessary. Hence, a basis must be established to maintain the affordability of the social security system in the Netherlands in the long term. The Government has, therefore, made proposals to limit the costs of pensions.

In this paper I discuss in succession the background and contents of the proposals in a general sense. Next, I deal more precisely with the proposals for the average career system. I then go on to discuss the proposals relating to mandatory industrial sector pension funds.

BACKGROUND AND CONTENTS OF THE PROPOSALS

Background of the Proposals

Affordability of Social Security

The proposals of the Government arise from concerns regarding the affordability of the social security system as a whole. It could be said that reliance on statutory social security benefits has increased enormously, or that the costs will rise considerably in the near future. The latter will certainly be the case with regard to the statutory basic old-age pension as from about the year 2010, due to ageing of the population.

Cost Control

The Government has ascertained that the costs of occupational pension schemes have also risen significantly for employers. This was due primarily to so-called 'back-service', as it is called in the Netherlands, which refers to the raising of past service pension commitments over past years of service if a rise in salary occurs. Therefore, the Government is in favour of the so-called average career system, in which the pension is a reflection of the salary earned during the entire career.

Flexibility and Mandatory Industrial Sector Pension Funds

In addition, the Government wants to promote flexibility in the area of pensions. The Government wants to realize such flexibility, among other ways, by limiting the costs of occupational pension schemes. With a view to flexibility, proposals are also being made to arrive at a limitation of the system of mandatory industrial sector pension schemes in the Netherlands.

The Third Pillar

The proposals in the document "Building for Security" do not concern the third pillar of the pension system. In mid-August 1997, however, it was made known that the Government wants to introduce a limitation on the tax deductibility of the premiums paid for a pension scheme in the third pillar. The Government believes that people are in a position to build up much too luxurious pensions.

THE PROPOSALS ON THE AVERAGE CAREER SYSTEM

Arguments Against the Final Pay System

The costs of salary-indexed occupational pension schemes based on final pay will rise considerably because of population ageing. Three reasons can be indicated for this.

First of all, it is caused by rising so-called past service commitments costs, in other words the rise in pension claims over past years of service. As a reflection of society as a whole, labour organizations also have to deal with an ageing staff, and the increase in the age profile is translated into higher pension costs.

Secondly, the number of pensioners – persons for whom the occupational old-age pension comes due – will rise significantly in the years to come. It is true that pensions in the Netherlands are financed with capital funds. However, this only applies to the pension payment as such and not to indexation of the pensions. Indexation will therefore have to come from premium payments and the proceeds of investments.

The third reason that the costs of occupational pension schemes will rise relates to ageing connected to the manner in which the occupational pension in the Netherlands is usually linked to the payment of the statutory basic pension (this is called the 'link'). Traditionally, the goal of many pension schemes has been to realize a pension replacement rate (including the statutory basic pension) of 70 per cent of final pay. If earnings are increasing faster than the amount of the statutory basic pension, then – in order to achieve the goal of 70 per cent – an increasingly large part of the total income from pensions will have to be financed via the occupational pension scheme.

The Government is thus faced with rising pension costs and therefore a rise in the costs of labour. This is a cause of great concern to the Government in view of the international competitive position of Netherlands trade and industry.

Argument for an Average Career System

Cost Control

It is for this reason that the Government has sought ways of limiting the costs of occupational pension schemes. The Government hopes to achieve this by promoting the creation of payments based on the average career instead of the final pay system.

The Government considers that a shift from final pay to average career systems will have a favourable effect on the costs of wages. In the long term this may also promote employment. Average career systems would also be better able to cope with ageing for the reasons indicated above.

An additional advantage, according to the Government, is that an average career system is more in keeping with the actual career pattern. Moreover, for people who have not made much of a career, the pension result in a final pay system will not be different compared to an average career system.

Flexibility

If the pension result can be limited via the average career system, this will make room for flexibility and individual freedom of choice in the area of pensions. Limitation of the pension result leaves the choice to the employee as to whether or not s/he takes out individual occupational pension insurance (third pillar). The higher pension result attached to a final pay system, however, will no longer apply collectively.

Modernization

Another consideration of the Government is the modernization of pension systems. The Government considers the final pay system to be too expensive, while a significant part of the costs to be incurred is necessary for the past service commitments of career makers.

Through saving costs by shifting to an average career system, the costs saved can be used for improving other elements of pensions, for example:

- offering a choice between old-age pension and survivors' pension. Particularly for the growing number of single people, as well as for double-income couples, this is an attractive option. The mandatory contribution and insurance for the survivors' pension will then be dropped;
- financing the possibility of an early pension;
- building up an occupational pension, including people with a lower salary (many occupational pension schemes now have a threshold salary of about NLG 30,000 per year. The employee can only build up an occupational pension with a salary above that amount).

In short, the introduction of an average career system would therefore also result in a redistribution of pension costs.

Tax Instrument

The Government wants to enforce the shift to average career systems through tax measures. The payment of premiums for an occupational pension scheme will be facilitated by tax measures, in other words they will not be part of taxable salary. At present the deduction of pension premiums from the salary is permitted, up to the level that is necessary to build up a final pay pension.

The Government would only like to allow the tax deductibility of pension premiums for average career systems.

Reaction of the Social Partners

The social partners (employers' and employees' organizations) and the pension fund organizations in the Netherlands have been severely critical of the Government's pension proposals.

They argue that the Government should not interfere with the formation of employment conditions. In addition, the introduction of an average career system as such would not limit the costs of labour, because then salary demands are to be expected.

Examination of the Proposal for Average Career Systems

The Average Career System Is Not Cheaper

The most important aspect is that the Government's assumption that an average career system is cheaper than a final pay system is incorrect. The pension result and with that pension costs are dependent upon many factors which are interconnected, such as:

- the percentage of pension build-up per year of service;
- the starting age for pension build-up;
- the starting age for pension payments;
- the amount of the salary from which level employees begin to build up occupational pension;
- the parts of the salary that count towards pension build-up (only fixed salary or bonuses, too?)
- the way in which the indexation of built-up claims is regulated.

Depending on the manner in which all these factors are interpreted, an average career system can result in better pension results – and thus be more expensive – than a final pay system. Practice in the Netherlands, whereby some companies have made the change from a final pay to an average career system, has also shown that the latter is not cheaper.

Modernization and Flexibility

It is indeed a fact that a distribution different to that of a final pay system creates room for the modernization and flexibility of pension schemes. Please refer to discussion of "flexibility" and "modernization" above.

Justified Intervention by the Government

The question is whether Government intervention in the occupational pension is justified. There may be doubts about this. The conditions of employment, including pensions, are the responsibility of the social partners. Shortly after the Second World War, the Netherlands had a so-called guided wage policy, in which the costs of wages in the framework of reconstruction were kept down by the Government. Since then, the formation of employment conditions and determination of the acceptable costs of labour (which includes pension costs) have been left to employers and employees themselves. Government intervention might be considered only if the results of consultations between employers and employees on pensions have socially undesirable consequences. However, it is difficult to label a final pay system as such an undesirable result.

Government intervention, however, would be conceivable on those points where Government measures are necessary to promote and supervise the creation and implementation of pension schemes. Among other things, this could involve facilitation through tax measures (not taxing pension premiums). For years it has been common practice to set boundaries on the extent to which pension premiums are eligible for tax deduction. The boundary is now set at pension premiums for a final pay pension. If, in connection with its steering policy, the Government finds it more effective to limit the tax deduction to premiums for an average career system, with regard to the delineation of their own tasks and responsibilities between the social partners on the one hand and the Government on the other, this would not raise too many objections.

Apart from that and in view of the criticism from the social partners, the Government has indicated that an average career pension in not a dogma and that therefore intervention in the pension result is no longer its primary option. The Government does find it very desirable that employees with a low salary (under NLG 30,000) are also able to build up an occupational pension. This is in the general interest of society as well, because the expectation is that the benefits for the statutory basic old-age pension could go down in the future. It is then desirable that employees begin earlier to build up occupational pension. Therefore the Government may want to make build-up over the lower salaries mandatory by law.

PROPOSALS FOR MANDATORY OCCUPATIONAL PENSION FUNDS

The System of Mandatory Industrial Sector Pension Funds in the Netherlands

The question of the need for Government measures for the implementation of occupational pension schemes also arises for the mandatory industrial sector pension funds.

The system of mandatory industrial sector pension funds works as follows. The social partners may decide in mutual consultation to establish an industrial sector pension fund, in other words, a pension fund for the employees in the specific sector of industry. There are, for example, pension funds for the metal industry, construction, health care, the textile industry etc. There are a total of over 80 of these industrial sector pension funds. However, participation in these industrial sector pension funds is, in principle, voluntary and only on a contractual basis. If it is made mandatory, the pension fund could yet acquire a generally binding effect in the specific industrial sector, so that all employees in that industrial sector would be legally obliged to participate, whether they want to or not. Making an industrial pension fund mandatory (declaring it generally binding) must be requested by the social partners from the Minister of Social Affairs and Employment, who may then decide to make it mandatory if s/he considers the social partners to be sufficiently representative of the entire industrial sector.

Of the more than 80 industrial pension funds in the Netherlands, more than 70 have been made mandatory in this manner. The mandatory industrial sector pension funds insure about 3.5 million employees, and they cover about 80 per cent of the active working population in the Netherlands. The quantitative significance of the mandatory industrial sector pension funds is therefore great.

Criticism of Mandatory Pension Funds: Unfair Competition?

Unfair Competition?

In recent years, especially on the part of insurance companies, there has been sharp criticism of the system of mandatory industrial sector pension funds. Insurers consider their mandatory nature to be a form of unfair competition and unacceptable monopoly. They also cite the EC Treaty which prohibits monopoly formation and competition-restricting agreements. Meanwhile, various proceedings are pending at the European Court of Justice in Luxembourg in which the question of the compatibility of mandatory industrial sector pension funds with the EC Treaty is at issue.

Restriction on Flexibility

In addition, mandatory participation in an industrial sector pension fund is considered by many companies to be an unnecessary restriction on the flexibility and freedom to set up a pension scheme at one's own discretion.

Obligation to Accept and General Interest

The industrial pension funds argue that they serve a general interest of society. Therefore, the industrial pension funds should not be designated as companies to which the EC Treaty applies, or mandatory participation in industrial sector pension funds should be justifiable in any case for social reasons (Article 90 EC Treaty).

The most important argument by far from the industrial sector pension funds as to why participation should be mandatory is that the funds are obliged to accept all employees without the possibility of medical examination or selection. That means automatically that a mandatory industrial pension fund is a mixture of good and bad risks, whereby the functioning of a mandatory industrial pension fund is based on solidarity between these groups. Such solidarity must, however, be supported. Without mandatory participation in the industrial pension funds, the good risks, those for whom the free insurance market is cheaper, would turn away from the funds. This would drain the pension fund with the ultimate effect that the bad risks could no longer be included in occupational pension schemes. Contrary to the mandatory industrial sector pension funds, insurance companies operate in a free market, where no obligation exists to conclude an insurance contract. This is the most important argument in favour of maintaining mandatory participation in industrial sector pension funds.

The Government's Standpoint on Mandatory Participation in Industrial Pension Funds

The Government endorses the social importance of the mandatory industrial sector pension funds, which is expressed in group solidarity. The cabinet therefore takes the standpoint that the instrument to make participation mandatory must be maintained.

However, the Government argues that the agreement of the social partners on the composition of a pension scheme within an industrial pension fund can no longer be followed automatically. In the framework of both the objective of cost control and intended flexibility, the Government is pursuing a limitation on the level of solidarity. In concrete terms, this mean that the Government will only cooperate in mandatory participation in an industrial pension fund up to a salary level of (approx.) NLG 75,000, which is equivalent to the salary level for which social insurance (disability, unemployment) is mandatory in the Netherlands. From the perspective of the its own responsibility, the Government does not see any arguments for making participation in an industrial pension fund mandatory for the higher salaries as well and imposing exacted solidarity on them. The viewpoint is that exacted solidarity here is not in the general interest of society.

Expanding the Possibility of Exemption

Another way in which the Government would like to open up the mandatory industrial pension funds is via the possibility of exemption. The regulation of the statutory system permits an industrial pension fund to exempt employees from the obligation to participate if their employer has arranged its own pension scheme. A condition for granting an exemption is that the employees build up pension claims under the other pension scheme for which the result is equal to the claims that would have been built up by participation in the industrial sector pension scheme.

The industrial pension funds are explicitly authorized to grant an exemption, and whether or not an exemption is granted is left to the funds' own policy judgement (with one exception: if the employer's own pension scheme already existed six months prior to submission of the request for exemption, the fund will be legally obliged to grant exemption).

The Government wants to arrive at a more detailed statutory description of the cases in which the pension fund is obliged to grant exemption. This would do more to meet the need for flexibility in the area of pensions. The Government wants to lay down a right to exemption in the following situations:

- the situation in which a company is part of a group of companies, while this group of companies does not fall under a mandatory industrial sector pension fund;
- the situation in which a company has been granted an exemption from a generally binding collective labour agreement and may therefore manage its own employment conditions policy;

- the situation in which the investment results of the pension fund are considered to be unsatisfactory on the basis of criteria to be formulated later in more detail.

In this way the Government wants to give substance to maintaining the social interest in industrial sector pension funds and simultaneously create room for more competition and more flexibility.

Assessment of the Proposals

In view of the fact that mandatory industrial sector pension funds function in a field of strongly conflicting and large commercial interests, it cannot be expected that the proposals of the Government will receive much support from the interested organizations. The insurance companies argue that the restrictions on the mandatory funds do not go far enough. The mandatory industrial pension funds argue that they already go too far, although it must be said here that the Government proposals follow a recommendation from the social partners on this issue.

Objectively speaking, I should think that the proposals attempt to find the proper stand midway between maintaining the social interest in mandatory participation and opening up more freedom and thus competition.

Conclusion

For years, the role of the State with respect to occupational pensions has been exercised at a distance. Occupational pensions are considered to belong to the territory of the social partners, part of the formation of employment conditions, and therefore a territory in which the Government should not interfere. In the past, Government policy with respect to occupational pensions was to create conditions and to stimulate pension provision. In that light, tax advantages from the payment of pension premiums and mandatory participation in industrial pension funds were regulated.

Today, an end seems to be coming to the "follower's role" that the Government has always taken. The Government wants to use the instruments of tax measures and mandatory participation to give substance to its own objectives and wishes in the area of pensions. Where this is in keeping with the primacy of the social partners to give substance to a pension system according to their own judgement, the proposals themselves are in tune with the philosophy that the social partners are primarily responsible for occupational pensions.

Part III THE STATE AS PENSION PROVIDER

11 DEMOGRAPHIC PROJECTIONS AND POPULATION AGEING IN IRELAND

Peter Connell and Jim Stewart

Introduction

Numerous studies and commentators have drawn attention to the forecast increase in the cost of old age pension provision, and possible future difficulties in funding pensions in many countries. The World Bank Report, Averting the Old Age Crisis, states in a much quoted foreword that:-

"Systems providing financial security for the old are under increasing strain throughout the world. Rapid demographic transitions caused by rising life expectancy and declining fertility mean that the proportion of old people in the general population is growing rapidly".

This chapter is in two parts. The first part considers recent forecasts of population and old age dependency ratios for Ireland (including those of the World Bank). Recent population forecasts are shown to be highly variable. In addition Ireland has in recent years experienced an economic boom (see Table 1). This boom, though largely unforecast is expected to result in above average growth rates for several more years. Higher than average growth has in turn led to considerable in-migration, in contrast to the historical experience of out-migration. This in turn has considerable implications for population growth and old age dependency ratios. The second part of the chapter considers these issues in the context of the affordability of old age pensions and the State pension system.

Table 1. Recent changes in GNP

Year	1992	1993	1994	1995	1996
% Change	2.1	2.9	7.6	8.0	6.9

Source: National Income and Expenditure, 1996, Dublin: Central Statistics Office, 1997.

Several studies in Ireland have also argued that demographic trends would result in considerable difficulties in financing future pension payments. For example, a study by the National Pensions Board in Ireland, (1993, p. 83) concluded that demographic trends would have a considerable negative impact in financing pay-as-you-go social welfare pensions as well as pensions in the non-commercial public sector. A document produced by the Department of Social Welfare and the National Pensions Board (1997, p. 35) summarises the National Pensions Board as predicting that between 1990 and 2035 the number of Social Insurance and Social Assistance pensioners would increase by 80% and the cost from *"13.9% to 25.1% of the taxable income of employees and the self employed"*. Others have broadly agreed with these conclusions. A report produced by a Government agency responsible for industrial development (Forfás Report, p. 19, 1996) states that although the proportion of the population aged 65 and over is expected to increase by only 1 or 2 % per annum in the next fifteen years, in the following 15 years it is expected to increase by 5.5% per annum. The report states that "this will place a significantly increased burden on the State pension system for which provision will require to be planned well in advance".

The World Bank Report has been criticised in Ireland and elsewhere for excessive pessimism in relation to the ability to fund future pension costs, and also for its policy prescriptions for future pension funding. Projected pension costs in Ireland prepared by the National Pensions Board (1993) have also been criticised (Fahey and FitzGerald 1997a, pp. 84-90). Research based on more recent migration data concludes that demographic trends in Ireland are less likely to pose economic problems. Fahey and FitzGerald (1997 a) conclude that "In Ireland exceptionally among western countries there will be considerable fewer dependants per worker in the future than in the recent past" and hence "the welfare state in Ireland should become more affordable in the years ahead than it has been at any time in the last three decades". Fahey and FitzGerald (1997 b) state (p. 27) that age dependency levels in Ireland are improving and "are likely to be lower in 30 years time than they were at various points in the last thirty years" and that the proportion of elderly in the population "will not show a major change till after 2010". This chapter considers these issues using the most recent census data available, published in July 1997, as well as migration data for the year 1997. This chapter also considers the implications of the demographic structures outlined for public pension costs and pension policy.

Demographic structures may influence costs of funding pension to the State and public sector pension costs in a number of ways. In recent years in Ireland an important part of social welfare pension policy has been to extend Social Insurance on a compulsory basis to all categories of the workforce and at the same time to increase the level of flat rate social security payments. For those who do not qualify for a contributory old age pension the policy has been to increase the overall level of flat rate social welfare payments including pensions (Pensions Board, 1998, p. 36). Hence the absolute size of the work force and population will have considerable implications for future pension costs. It should be noted that State and occupational pensions are considered jointly in order to achieve a generally accepted replacement rate of 66%. In practice what this means is that an increase in State pensions reduces occupational pension payments with consequent savings to employers (National Pensions Board, p. 102).

Population structures also have considerable implications for demand for State services, for example health services with an ageing population and hence the numbers and costs, including pension costs, of public sector employees[1]. This is true even if public sector pensions are funded or unfunded. Tax reliefs on funded pension schemes within the public sector could be regarded as an internal transfer – the tax reliefs result in less current government payments to fund future pensions.

2. 1996 Census Results and Population Forecasts for 1996

Table 2 shows that several forecasts underestimated the population for 1996. A key reason for this was the assumption of net out-migration in the period 1991-96, rather than the recorded net inflow of 8300 (CSO, 1997 Table K). For the intercensal period 1991-96 the National Pensions Board (1993, p. 245) assumed net out migration of 25,000; Connell projections in Fahey (1995, p. 28) assumed net out migration of 40,000, The Central Statistics Office (1995) assume a likely range of outflows from 37,500 to 87,500.

Table 2. Census Estimates of Population, Labour Force and Dependency Ratios for 1996 Compared with Previous Forecasts ('000).

Source	Population	Labour Force[1]	Numbers Aged 65+	Demographic[2] Dependency	Old Age Dependency
National Pensions Board 1993			402		
CSO, 1995 Low migration & high fertility[3]	3588	1433.8	411	53.6	17.6
Connell projections in Fahey, 1995	3590		415		
CSO Labour Force Survey, 1996	3621	1475.0	415	54.6	17.7
Census	**3626**		**414**	**54.1**	**17.6**

Notes to Table 2.
(1) Apart from demographic assumptions labour force projections will vary according to assumptions about participation rates.
(2) Defined as the sum of those aged less than 15 plus those aged 65+ divided by those aged 15-64
(3) This is the most optimistic forecast.

Projections

Table 3 shows our forecast projections. As noted above population projections for Ireland have not been accurate in the past because of highly variable migratory flows. Hughes (1996a) remarks "population projections are subject to considerable margins of error and the error is likely to increase with the length of the projection period". Fahey and FitzGerald (1997a, p. 8) consider that even short period projections may be unreliable. Population projections for countries without large and unpredictable migratory flows are likely to be more accurate, but nevertheless are unreliable over long periods[2].

Table 3. 1996 Population and Forecasts of Population and Old Age Dependency Ratios for the Period 2001-2031 ('000)

Year	1996	2001	2006	2011	2016	2021	2026	2031
0-14	859	806	796	808	798	760	708	658
15-64	2353	2546	2668	2727	2750	2762	2748	2699
65+	414	422	450	508	593	675	758	838
Total Population	3626	3776	3914	4043	4141	4198	4214	4195
Demographic[1] Dependency Ratio	54.1	48.2	46.7	48.3	50.6	52.0	53.3	55.4
Old Age[2] Dependency Ratio	17.6	16.6	16.9	18.6	21.6	24.4	27.6	31.0
Labour Force	1489	1675	1800	1843	1838	1817	1789	1747
Old Age Economic[3] Dependency Ratio	27.8	25.2	25.0	27.6	32.3	37.1	42.4	48.0

Note: (1) Defined as those aged 0-14 plus those aged 65+ divided by those aged 15-64 and expressed in per cent.
(2) Defined as those aged 65+ divided by those aged 15-64 (per cent).
(3) Those aged 65+ divided by the labour force (per cent).

The key points from Table 3 are: -
(1) The forecast population increases until the year 2026 and then falls.
(2) The number of those aged 65+ also increases in every period from 414,000 in 1996 to 838,000 in 2031. The forecast absolute number of those aged 65+ is higher in each census year compared with previous forecasts. For example the National Pensions Board (1993) forecast 569,000 over 65s for the year 2021. However the forecasts in Table 3 show that the old age dependency ratio is lower in 2006 than 1996, and then rises to 31% of the adult population by 2031. It is interesting to note that forecast old age dependency ratios in this chapter are slightly lower than those forecast by the National Pensions Board (1993) although both the number of those aged 65+ and total population are forecast to be considerably higher.
(3) The demographic dependency ratio (including those aged 0-14 in the numerator) falls from 54% to 46.7% in 2006 and then rises to 55.4% in 2031. Thus there is little difference in the overall demographic dependency ratio comparing 1996 with 2031;

(4)   The labour force also increases in every period until 2011. The absolute size of the labour force and the rate of growth of the labour force are thus substantially larger than previous forecasts.

(5)   Despite the rapid increase in those aged 65+ the ratio of those aged 65+ to the labour force is slightly lower in 2011 compared with 1996 (27.6% versus 27.8%). The ratio increases rapidly thereafter to 48% by 2031.

The implications of various measures of demographic dependency are further discussed in the context of pension costs in section 7.

A key difference between the forecasts in this chapter and previous forecasts (shown in Table 4) is the assumption that there will be net in-migration to Ireland in future periods. Previous forecasts assumed net outflows. For example the National Pensions Board (1993) assumed outflows of 20,000 in the period 1996-2001, falling to outflows of 5000 in the period 2021-2026. Forfás (1996) assume out-migration of over 11,000 each year until the year 2005 and 3,400 thereafter. FitzGerald and Fahey (1997) assume zero migration during the period 1997-2005 (p. 132) with emigration resuming after the year 2005 (Figure 2.23). Forecasts contained in an actuarial review of the future cost of Social Welfare Pensions assume zero net migration (Actuarial Review, 1997, p. 47). While the projections in this chapter assume net in-migration this is made up of flows into Ireland in the age group 0-14, outflows in the age group 15-24 and inflows in the age groups 25-44, with smaller inflows in age groups 45+. Section (3) below discusses the basis for migration assumptions. Other assumptions in the forecasts are similar to those in the population projections by Connell in Fahey (1995). One exception is a further assumed increase in life expectancy in the period 1996 to 2011 compared with earlier periods. Irish life expectancy rates for those aged 65+ have historically been well below the EU average. Since 1986 life expectancy for those aged 65+ has increased in Ireland. This chapter assumes that this increase will continue at the same rate until the year 2016. Increased life expectancy is partly responsible for the forecast growth in numbers in those aged 65+.

Why Inward Migration?

Our assumptions about net inward migration produce quite different forecasts of future population and dependency ratios and hence it is worth spending a little time considering these assumptions.

Honohan (1992) in particular emphasises the key role of migration flows in explaining Irish unemployment rates. Honohan states (p.38): -

"The underlying model behind the statistical equations is that there exists a pool of workers located on both sides of the Irish sea, who have a preference for living in Ireland and who will migrate to (or stay in) Ireland if unemployment conditions are not too bad there relative to conditions in the U.K.".

The National Economic and Social Council (NESC 1991, p. 160) states: -

"For many of the better educated middle class.... emigration appears to be seen as a normal option in career planning".

Table 4. Recent Population Forecasts ('000)

Year	2001	2006	2011	2016	2021	2026	2031	2036
National Pensions Board 1993	3481		3424		3361		3270	3210
CSO, 1995 Low migration & high fertility[1]	3649	3719	3832	3934	4013	4068		
Connell projections in Fahey, 1995	3622	3652	3693					
FitzGerald , 1995	3551	3528						
Forfás, 1996[2]	3585	3574	3594					
ESRI: Fahey & Fitzgerald, 1997	3704	3782	3886					
DKM in National Pensions Policy Initiative, 1997[3]		3762		3936		4028		3995
Actuarial Review, 1997		3832		4012	4089		4071	
Forecast 1998	**3776**	**3914**	**4043**	**4141**	**4198**	**4214**	**4195**	

(1) This forecast is based on the most optimistic assumptions;
(2) Population projections relate to the year 2000, 2005 and 2010;
(3) DKM economic consultants prepared the forecast.

The NESC report also comments:-

"That the typical returning emigrant is about 10 years older than the typical emigrant. He or she is more likely to be married and have children. It is also probable that (s) he has accumulated some financial capital, work experience and skills during the stay abroad".

More recently Barrett and Trace (1998) in a study of the educational profile of population inflows conclude, "that recently returned migrants have higher educational profile than the resident population".

Table 4 shows estimated migratory flows for the intercensal period 1991-1996 and also for the period 1971-81 for comparative purposes. This latter period also experienced net in-migration. For 1991-96 the table shows relatively large net outflows in the age group 15-24, with net inflows in the age groups 25-44. Smaller relative inflows take place in the age groups 45-65 and 65+ reflecting a long established trend. The other notable feature is the net inflows in the age group 0-14 (amounting to 8% of births during this period) reflecting the return of family groups.

Our forecasts assume the trends of net in migration for the period 1991-96 shown in Table 5, will be repeated in future periods, that is continuing in migration in the 0-14 age group, net out migration in the age-group 15-24, net in migration in the 25-34 age group, and 35-44 age group, with relatively smaller inflows in the age groups 45-64 and 65+. These inflows are assumed to take place in response to forecast growth rates and job opportunities (Conniffe et al Medium Term Review, 1997, Table 6.2) [3.] The ESRI Medium Term Review forecasts (p. 107) that GNP is likely to grow by 5.5% per annum in the period 1995-2000, by 5% in the period 2000-2005 and by 4% in the period 2005-2010. In this chapter in-migration is assumed to amount to a net inflow of 60,000 persons for the period 1996-2001, in response to strong economic growth. In-migration is assumed to fall to 30,000 in the period 2001-2006, to fall further to 20,000 in the period 2006-2011 and to amount to 10,000 per intercensal period thereafter. Inflows are assumed to fall from more recent levels as costs increase in the domestic economy reducing demand for labour. Ireland's relatively high income per capita is however likely to result in a continuing flow of immigration. These inflows combined with higher participation rates by married women will result in a growing labour force. Forecasts of future GNP growth have associated predictions of a fall in unemployment rates. Hence given a growing labour force and a fall in unemployment rates it is reasonable to assume that most returnees are employed rather than unemployed. The Medium Term Review (Conniffe et al, p. 165) notes that there is likely to be a change in the nature of migratory flows as income levels in Ireland exceed the EU average. It is possible that in the latter part of the forecast period the nature of in-migration will change. Rather than Irish born immigrants returning, in-migration flows will also include those from other EU countries as well as non-EU countries. In part this in-migration, as in other developed European economies (see NESC, 1991, Table 2.7), will be in response to job opportunities in low wage employment.

Migration flows in response to Tax/transfer Payments

The relative value of social welfare payments comparing Ireland and the U.K. has changed dramatically in the period 1979 to date. Table 4.4 of Callan and Sutherland (1997) shows that unemployment benefit and old age benefit payments were higher in Ireland in 1994/95 than in the U.K. reversing the historic differential. While Table 4.1 of Callan and Sutherland shows that tax rates are higher in Ireland compared with the U.K. These authors note (p. 99) the possible impact of tax/transfer policy on migration flows are complex. Nevertheless they say (p. 99) that:-

(1)   To the extent that the emphasis in the UK on work incentives led to greater employment creation than in Ireland there may be migration from Ireland;

(2)   For those with job options in either country tax cuts in the UK may result in migration from Ireland;

(3)   They state: "the rise in welfare rates in Ireland relative to the UK may have lessened the stimulus to emigrate for those seeking work, or induced a return to Ireland among some Irish emigrants who became unemployed in the UK."

Table 5. Migration by Age Cohort for the period 1991-96 and 1971-81 ('000) and
Forecast for the period 1996-2001

Age	Net flow 1991-96	Net flow 1971-81	Forecast Net flow 1996-2001
0 - 4			2.5
5 - 9			10.0
10-14			8.0
0-14	20.1	47.4	20.5
15-19			-5.0
20-24			-26.0
15-24	-48.9	-10.2	-31.0
25-29		-7.0	-1.0
30-34		20.0	25.0
25-34	9.0	-1.1	24.0
35-39			20.0
40-44			8.0
35-44	12.0	39.6	28.0
45-49			2.5
50-54			2.5
45-54	4.6	10.2	5.0
55-59			2.0
60-64			3.0
55-64	5.5	-0.4	5.0
65+	5.9	18.2	5.0
Total Inflow	**8.3**	**103.9**	**60.0**
Annual Inflow	**1.66**	**10.4**	**12.0**

Source: CSO, 1996, Table K.

Previous research has also indicated a possible link between changes in the
structure of social welfare and income tax in Britain and Ireland affecting migration.
NESC (1991) concludes (p. 124) that recent changes "have disproportionately
increased the incentives for those with relatively high earnings potential to
emigrate"[4].

If only those aged 65+ are considered the latest census data show a drop in
annual migration into Ireland of those aged 65+ (5,900 compared with 7,200 in the
period 1986-91). If as argued by Fahey (1995, p. 25) the level of in-migration by
those aged 65+ was underrecorded in earlier years, the long term trend downwards

may be more pronounced. Given forecast trends in labour force growth (upwards) and unemployment (downwards) adult inflows are likely to be largely employed rather than being reliant on social welfare payments. The recent census results are consistent with our assumption of a change in the pattern of migration flows. Given these strong behavioural preferences (apart from possible macroeconomic effects resulting from changes in tax/transfer regimes), it is likely that transfer payments and tax rates would be required to diverge substantially between Ireland and the U.K. before such differentials would induce migration flows.

Some Implications

A number of interesting demographic implications follow if the forecasts in Table 2 reflect future trends. For example the number of school-going children and child dependency rates are higher than those predicted from the crude birth rate because of the return of adults with children (hence school population declines more slowly). Furthermore because of net inflows in the age groups 25+, the absolute number of births is forecast to increase slightly in the period to 2006. The increased births recorded in 1996 and 1997 (to date) compared with 1994-95 support this assumption. It is assumed migratory flows largely occur in the age groups 0-44 and that as discussed previously, following the postwar trend there are relatively few in-migrants aged 65+.

NESC concluded (1991, p. 37) that "the relative age structure of emigrants and immigrants imparts a higher dependency ratio to the population than would naturally occur"

Following from our assumptions net migration reduces the overall dependency ratio slightly because of the return of the economically active. The old age dependency ratio is also reduced. Table (3) shows the forecast old age dependency ratio falling from 17.6% in 1996 to 16.6% in 2001, rising gradually until 2011 and at a faster rate to 31% by the year 2031. In the context of the life cycle savings model it is also likely that in-migrants have accumulated financial assets, including pension rights[5]. Thus in-migration may also be associated with personal financial flows into Ireland.

How Are Demographic Projections Linked to Pension Costs?

Population projections in this chapter confirm other forecasts that there will be an increase in the numbers of those aged 65+. This increase is gradual up until 2006 at less than 1% per annum and increases thereafter at a rate of 2-3% per annum. The forecast number of those aged 65+ in this chapter is larger that forecast by the National Pensions Board in 1993, (Table 7) and hence absolute costs are likely to be higher. If projected expenditures on social welfare pensions by the National Pensions Board are expressed in 1996 prices they would amount to £2671 million for the year 2030 compared with projected expenditure of £1573 million in 1995. The most recent actuarial review of social welfare pensions (Irish Pensions Trust, 1997, p. 21) estimates that in constant prices total social welfare pension payments will increase from £1707 million in 1996 to £3152 million in 2026 and £3738 million in 2036. The increase is even larger if pension payments are increased in line with projected average earnings.

PAYG public sector pension costs amounted to £569 million in 1996 (National Pensions Policy Initiative, p. 35). Even without changes in pension rates and conditions future costs will rise because of the age-profile of employees, 55.1% of public sector employees are in the age group 35-55 (Source: Special tabulation of 1996 Labour Force Survey). Apart from PAYG pension costs there will also be pension costs arising from the need to meet pension commitments in funded schemes such as Telecom Eireann and An Post[6]. Actuarial estimates of the size of fund (and annual payments) required to meet future public sector pension costs are very large (see for example Joyce, Reilly and Smythe, 1995, p. 17; Turner and Rajnes, 1997, p. 18).

Actuarial estimates of the present value or future value of costs will vary (as do population projections) depending on the assumptions chosen, for example the level of payout, or the discount rate for future liabilities (Joyce, Reilly, Smythe, p. 11 & p. 16). There is also a link between actuarial estimates and demographic estimates. Demographic changes such as increased life expectancy also affect actuarial cost estimates. It is likely for example that the trend in mortality rates for general civil service pension schemes reflects the trend in mortality rates in the population as whole.

As noted earlier the growth in the cost of social welfare pensions through extension of coverage and higher payments has considerable implications for funded schemes because of the policy of coordination or integration. The higher the basic State pension the lower the cost to employers. The converse is also true (National Pensions Policy Initiative 1997, p. 36).

Dependency ratios (for example the ratio of those aged less than 15 plus those aged 65+ to those aged 15-64) may also provide a useful guide to the ability to finance future pension costs. This is likely to be the case irrespective of whether the pension system is funded or PAYG. As Joyce, Reilly, Smythe state p. 13) if the ability of the State to raise taxes were called into question "the security of any assets built up in a fund would be equally dubious".

Our forecasts show a stable demographic dependency ratio comparing 1996 with 2031, but also show a rising old age dependency ratio. A stable overall demographic dependency ratio may not imply stable proportionate costs, for example children and old people may not have identical dependency levels and associated costs (Fahey and FitzGerald, 1997a p. 14). There may be large differences in dependency levels (and associated costs) between those aged 65-85 and those aged 85+[7].

When considering future costs and ability to finance future pension arrangements it is important to consider not only demographic old age dependency (gerontic ratios) but also various measures of economic dependency. One widely used economic dependency ratio measure relates the numbers of those aged 65+ to the labour force.

Apart from demographic factors the size of the labour force will be partly determined by participation rates (for example changes in higher education patterns, increased participation by married women). Higher female participation rates and lower unemployment rates are forecast to increase the size of the work force in future years. One factor, which may work in the opposite direction, is a trend towards retirement prior to age 65. According to evidence cited by Disney (p. 197) for the UK for those not covered by occupational or private pension arrangements the "rate of exit into inactivity" is constant for those aged 40+ reflecting ill health, redundancy etc. Whereas for those aged 40+ in private pension schemes the probability of continuing to work is downward sloping. Disney explains this finding by saying that those covered by occupational/private sector pension schemes work until the first date at which they become eligible for early retirement provisions, which will be a function of scheme rules. For the U.K. the proportion of those aged 55-65 at work has fallen from 75% in 1978 to 42% in 1993. Tanner (1998) explains this by the growth in retirement rather than unemployment. Disney cites evidence (pp. 193-195) for declining participation rates for men aged between 55-64 in a number of OECD countries and recommends (p. 199) "a structure of economic incentives that persuades the potential worker to continue working". In order to be effective such economic incentives would need to be accompanied by considerable institutional change.

There are other measures of economic dependency. Falkingham (1989) for example computes various measures of demographic dependency and economic dependency for the UK calculated using differing measures of the 'dependent population' divided by a number of differing measures of the 'working population'. She produces two measures of economic dependency. Ratio B adjusts all age cohorts of the population for economic activity. Those who are available for work are defined as economically active. This means that for those aged 65+ for 1981 23.9 % of men and 9.5% of women were defined as economically active. Ratio C further adjusts this estimate of the economically active for unemployment and sickness. Those who are unemployed or sick are removed from the denominator and included in the numerator as part of the 'dependent population'. Falkingham shows that while economic dependency ratios are higher than demographic dependency ratios during the period 1951 1981 demographic dependency rose from 0.73 to 0.86, ratio B fell from 1.18 to 1.11, and ratio C rose from 1.21 to 1.34 largely reflecting growing unemployment during this period[7].

Table 6 shows various measures of economic dependency. For comparative purposes demographic and old age dependency are also shown. As expected estimates of economic dependency are higher than gerontic dependency. Table (5) shows that estimates of economic dependency can vary substantially. For example Ratio 5 which shows old age economic dependency adjusted for those who are economically active (that is, those who are aged 65+ and economically active are removed from the numerator), is 19% lower than Ratio 6 for 1996 and 9% lower in 2031. Ratio (6) is defined as old age dependency expressed as a per cent of those at work (the labour force less those unemployed).

Table 7 shows previous forecasts of Old Age Dependency ratios compared with our forecast. Compared with other forecasts the forecast old age dependency ratio is lower up to the year 2011 and then rises, so that for the year 2026 and for later years it is similar to other long-range forecasts.

Table 6. Forecasts of Population and Old Age Dependency ratios for the Period 2001-2031 (per cent)

Year	1996	2001	2006	2011	2016	2021	2026	2031
(1) Demographic dependency	54.1	48.2	46.7	48.3	50.6	52.0	53.4	55.4
(2) Old Age dependency	17.6	16.6	16.9	18.6	21.7	24.5	27.5	31.0
(3) Adjusted old age dependency	21.0	19.0	19.0	21.0	24.0	27.0	30.0	34.0
(4) Old Age Economic dependency	27.8	25.2	25.0	27.5	32.3	37.1	42.4	48.0
(5) Adjusted old age economic dependency	25.6	23.4	23.4	26.1	30.9	35.6	40.6	46.0
(6) Old age dependency as a ratio of Labour force minus unemployed	31.5	27.6	26.8	29.3	34.0	39.1	44.6	50.5

Definitions

(1) The ratio of those aged 0-14 plus those aged 65+ to those aged 15-64
(2) The ratio of those aged 65+ to those aged 15-64
(3) The ratio of those aged 65+ to those aged 20-64
(4) The ratio of those aged 65+ to the forecast labour force
(5) The ratio of those aged 65+ less those aged 65+ economically active to the labour force
(6) The ratio of those aged 65+ to the labour force less forecast unemployment rates from ESRI Medium Term Review (1997, Table 6.10) for the years to 2011 and assumed at 5% for later periods.

The World Bank shows old age dependency ratios for those aged over 60+ for all countries in the world for ten year intervals for the period 1990- 2150. For comparative purposes Table 1 (appendix) shows this data for OECD countries for the years 1990-2030. Forecast dependency ratios reach a peak for Austria, Germany, Luxembourg, the Netherlands and Switzerland in 2030. The World Bank shows Irelands dependency ratio reaching a peak in the year 2150 at 30.9! On World Bank projections Ireland can be seen to have the lowest dependency ratio of the countries shown for the year 2030. Using forecasts from this chapter the trend in Irish dependency ratios is slightly higher than those forecast by the World Bank. Because of differing demographic profiles policy prescriptions for other countries may not be appropriate in the Irish context.

Table 7. Forecasts of Old Age Dependency Ratios

Year	2001	2006	2011	2016	2021	2026	2031	2036
National Pensions Board 1993	18.1		20.1		26.4		31.7	33.5
CSO, 1995 Low migration & high fertility	17.1	17.4	18.7	21.1	23.7	26.3		
Connell Projections, in Fahey 1995	18.0	19.1	19.1					
ESRI: Fahey & Fitzgerald, 1997	17.1	17.3	18.7					
Forecast 1998	**16.6**	**16.9**	**18.6**	**21.6**	**24.4**	**27.6**	**31.0**	**34.0**

Note: Old age demographic dependency ratios are calculated as the ratio of those
        aged 65+ to age groups 15-64.

Economic dependency ratios give a better indication of the future costs of pension arrangements but still suffer a number of drawbacks. According to Disney (1996, p. 25) "...the driving factor in raising the burden of social security pensions in many Western countries is not the trend in dependency so much as the trend in the real value of social security". Hughes (1996, Table 2) shows that if real GNP were assumed to grow at 2% per annum, and Social Welfare Pension Costs are indexed to prices and are as forecast by the National Pensions Board (1993, p. 37), then social welfare pensions would fall from 5.0% in 1990 to 4.1% of GNP in 2035.

As noted earlier a growing number of those aged 65+ will result in an increase in absolute pension costs. Whether the large forecast increase in absolute payments results in higher tax levels will depend on replacement rates chosen, and on whether payments are indexed to wages or prices. In addition, as others have suggested other State financed expenditures may fall. Whether projected absolute cost increases result in higher tax rates also depends on growth in GNP and wage levels. For example a recent report by the Pensions Board (1998, Table 4.6) shows that holding certain variables constant, assuming social welfare pensions costs are indexed to earnings and assuming a 2.9% increase in GNP per annum rather than 3.4% payments would rise from 4.5% in 1998 to 13.9% of GNP by the year 2056. Higher costs may require policy changes. Hughes (1996b, p. 58) notes "Governments face considerable difficulties in securing agreement on which groups in the population should bear the cost, as the recent history of pension reform in Italy and France shows". This chapter has shown that population projections can be quite uncertain. Projections of future growth in wages and GNP are even more uncertain. There may be also be further uncertainty as to the size of the tax base in forecast GNP, because of the large multinational company sector in Ireland and possible capital mobility in response to tax changes.

Conclusions

Population forecasts in this chapter show that the number of those aged 65+ will increase by over 100% between 1996 and 2031. This is a greater number than forecast by for example the National Pensions Board. However old age dependency ratios will not rise to the same extent during the forecast period. Demographic dependency ratios are similar comparing 1996 and 2031 (54.1% compared with 55.4%). Our forecasts show that the per cent of the population aged 60 years and over will be lower in Ireland by the year 2020 than in Germany by the year 2000 (see appendix).

Population and labour force projections are a valuable basis for policy formation, but policy makers must also note the considerable uncertainty associated with population forecasts. It is safe to conclude that there will be growing numbers of those aged 65+ in the Irish population. This may result in a number of changes to current pension systems. Policy options which encourage low unemployment and economic success are likely to be more important in ensuring that future pension costs can be financed than the precise form of the pension system. An additional area that may require changes, based not just on economic criteria, would be to develop policies with the aim of keeping a greater number of those aged 65+ economically active.

When considering the relative costs of pension systems economic dependency is more relevant than demographic dependency. Here there is very little change comparing 1996 and 2011. Economic dependency ratios are forecast to rise after 2011 and are between 40% and 60% higher by 2026. The largest intercensal increase is forecast to take place between 2026 and 2031. The extent to which a rise in old age economic dependency rates poses an economic problem will depend on the trend in relative future pension costs, for example replacement rates for social security based pensions, or forecast future public sector employees, age at retirement and the relative growth of pensionable wages in the public sector.

Notes

1. A Government Commission is currently enquiring into the costs of public sector pensions in Ireland
2. In this regard it is interesting to note that the World Bank Report (1994) forecasts demographic dependency ratios for those aged 60+ for all countries in the world (including Ireland) up until the year 2150.
3. The Financial Times (15/2/97) reported that the Construction Industry Federation is attempting to persuade 5000 workers to return to Ireland, and that a successful campaign could cause a skills shortage in the UK.
4. Although the NESC report also states (p. 159) that "It is the expected or actual failure to achieve employment (occupational) aspirations locally that is the main personal motive explaining migration intentions and behaviour", and that "Income dissatisfaction, though much less important than occupational attainment, does however, constitute an independent source of migration motivations".
5. See Attanasio (1997) for a recent discussion of theory and empirical evidence relating to this model.
6. Payments to these two schemes from the Minister for Finance for the year 1993 amounted to £39 m. and £37 m. for 1992. On occasion other pension liabilities arise where funded schemes in the public sector are insufficient to meet actual payments, for example in the case of the universities, where pension payment are indexed to final salary but schemes are funded on the basis of no increase in pension payments.

7. Falkingham (1989, p. 217) states that for the UK "The different age groups that comprise the elderly population exert differential demands on the health and social services, with those aged 85 and over being the most expensive group per capita, and over half of hospital beds now being occupied by those aged over 75".

8. These data are taken from Disney (1996) p. 25.

Appendix

Table 1. World Bank Data Showing Percentage of the Population over sixty years old 1990-2030 (per cent)

	1990	2000	2010	2020	2030
Australia	15.0	15.3	18.1	22.8	27.7
Austria	20.2	21.5	24.9	28.9	34.5
Belgium	20.7	22.5	24.8	28.7	32.2
Canada	15.6	16.8	20.4	25.9	30.2
Denmark	20.2	20.4	24.8	28.4	32.1
Finland	18.4	19.8	24.4	28.7	30.9
France	18.9	20.2	23.1	26.8	30.1
Germany	20.3	23.7	26.5	30.3	35.3
Greece	20.2	24.2	26.5	29.1	32.5
Iceland	14.5	14.9	17.3	21.4	26.0
Ireland	15.2	15.7	17.8	20.1	22.9
Ireland* (own forecast)	**15.2**	**15.1**	**17.8**	**22.0**	**26.1**
Italy	20.6	24.2	27.4	30.6	35.9
Japan	17.3	22.7	29.0	31.4	33.0
Luxembourg	19.3	21.2	25.3	29.5	33.0
Netherlands	17.8	19.0	23.4	28.4	33.4
New Zealand	15.2	15.9	18.9	22.7	26.8
Portugal	18.0	19.8	21.4	24.6	29.7
Spain	18.5	20.6	22.4	25.6	30.9
Sweden	22.9	21.9	25.4	27.8	30.0
Switzerland	19.9	21.9	26.6	30.5	34.0
United Kingdom	20.8	20.7	23.0	25.5	29.6
United States					
Simple average	18.6	20.0	23.2	26.9	30.8
Weighted average	18.2	19.9	23.1	27.0	30.7

Source: World Bank (1994), Table A.2.
* Refers to the years 2001, 2011, 2021 and 2031.

References

Attanasio, O. "Consumption and Saving Behaviour: Modelling Recent Trends", *Fiscal Studies*, vol. 18, no. 1, pp. 23-47, 1997.

Barrett, A. and Trace, F. "Who is Coming Back? The Educational Profile of Returning Migrants in the 1990s, *Irish Banking Review*, pp. 38-51, Summer, 1998

Callan, T. and Sutherland, H. "Income Supports in Ireland and the U.K.", in *Income Support and Work Incentives: Ireland and the U.K.* Tim Callan (ed.) Dublin: E.S.R.I. 1997.

Central Statistics Office. *Population and Labour Force Projections 1996-2016*, Dublin: Central Statistics Office, Pn 1455, 1995.

Central Statistics Office, *Labour Force Survey 1996*, Dublin: CSO, pn 3442, 1997

Central Statistics Office, *Census 96. Principal Demographic Results*, Dublin: CSO, Pn 4167, 1997.

Commission on Public Sector Pensions. *Interim Report to the Minister for Finance*, Dublin: Commission on Public Sector Pensions, 1997.

Department of Social Welfare and The Pensions Board. *National Pensions Policy Initiative Consultation Document*, Dublin: The Pensions Board, 1997.

Disney, R. *Can We Afford to Grow Older?* London: MIT Press, 1996.

Fahey, T. *Health and Social Care Implications of Population Ageing in Ireland*, 1991-2011, Dublin: National Council for the Elderly, Report no. 42, 1995.

Fahey, T and FitzGerald, J. *Welfare Implications of Demographic Trends*, Dublin: Oak Tree Press in association with Combat Poverty Agency, 1997a.

Fahey, T and FitzGerald, J. "The Educational Revolution and Demographic Change", in Duffy, D. FitzGerald, J, Kearney, I. and Shorthall, (1997), *The Medium Term Review: 1997-2003*, Dublin: Economic and Social Research Institute, 1997b.

Falkingham, J."Dependency and Ageing in Britain: A Re-Examination of the Evidence", *Journal of Social Policy*, vol. 18, no. 2 pp. 2111-233, 1989.

FitzGerald, J. "Babies, Budgets and the Bathwater, *Irish Banking Review*, Summer, pp. 18-32, 1995

Forfás. *Shaping Our Future. A Strategy for Enterprise in Ireland in the 21st Century*, Dublin: Forfás, 1996.

Honohan, P." The Link Between Irish and UK Unemployment", *Quarterly Economic Commentary*, Spring, pp. 33-44, 1992.

Hughes, G. "Would Privatising Pensions Increase Savings?" *Irish Banking Review*, pp. 28-42, *Spring*, 1996a.

Hughes, G. "Pension Financing, the Substitution Effect and National Saving", *Proceedings of the conference on Pensions in the European Union: Adapting to Economic and Social Changes*, Munster, Germany, June 13-16, 1996b.

Irish Pensions Trust. *Actuarial Review of Social Welfare Pensions*, Dublin: Stationery Office, 1997.

Joyce, J. Reilly I. and Smythe, R. " Public Sector Pension Provision", paper given to the Societies of Actuaries of Ireland, Conrad Hotel, 23rd November 1995.

NCB Stockbrokers. *Population and Prosperity Sustaining the Boom*, Dublin: NCB, 1998.

National Economic and Social Council. *The Economic and Social Implications of Emigration*, Report no. 90, Pl 7840 Dublin: NESC, 1991.

National Pensions Board. *Developing the National Pension System*, Dublin: Stationery Office, 1993.

Pensions Board. *Securing Retirement Income*, Pensions Board, Dublin, 1998.

Tanner, S. "The Dynamics of Male Retirement Behaviour", *Fiscal Studies*, vol. 19, no. 2 pp. 175-196, 1998.

Turner, J.A. and Rajnes D.M. "Reform of Pensions for Federal Government Employees in the United States". This volume, 1998.

World Bank. *Averting the Old Age Crisis*, Oxford: Oxford University Press, 1994.

12 THE EFFECTS OF INDEXATION REFORM ON OLD-AGE PENSION BENEFITS AND PENSION EXPENDITURE IN FINLAND

Toini Christiansson

Introduction

Due to rising dependency rates, the lengthening of life expectancy, and economic prospects, the indexation of pensions is a very topical issue. The pension adjustment deals with the necessity to maintain the buying power of retirement incomes. Automatic indexation of pension benefits and revaluation of pensionable basic income are common in most industrialised countries. Without upward revaluation, inflation reduces the real value of the pensionable income. The pension benefits and the pensionable basic salary can be indexed to prices or wages or to some combination of both.

The indexation mechanism is an essential part of the implicit social contract between the generation of active workers and that of pensioners. It is an insurance against future unexpected changes in inflation or in income levels. Over many years even minor changes of adjustment rules produce large effects on the transfer ratio.

PAYG-schemes use one or more of the following indexation mechanisms:

- automatic revaluation to maintain the purchasing power of pensions by indexing them to prices,
- automatic revaluation to maintain the ratio of pensions to wages by indexing the former to the latter,
- evaluation by discretionary measures on the part of the authorities.

Indexation can be used as an instrument for the following four purposes: a) value adjustment of pensionable basic income, b) calculating the beginning pension benefit, c) revaluing the running pension benefit and d) adjustment of the ceiling for pensionable basic income. The instrument for indexation is of importance for pension benefits, the consumption power of the retired population, the balance between the pensioner's and the active population's disposable income, and pension expenditure.

In most OECD-countries the pensionable basic income is revalued by a wage index. A price index is used as the only adjustment instrument in Sweden, Spain,

Italy and Luxembourg. In Finland, Norway and Belgium the pensionable income is revalued by a combination of price and wage indices. The ceiling for pensionable income is usually adjusted by the same index as is the pensionable income. Finland is the only country in Western Europe that has not yet introduced a ceiling for the pensionable income under legislated supplementary pension schemes.

The indexation of pension benefits in the OECD-countries is most often linked to a price index. The pension adjustment by a wage index or a combined index is also common. There are only a few countries in Western Europe that are without an automatic pension adjustment: Denmark (supplementary pension), Ireland, Switzerland (supplementary pension) and Portugal. In Finland the indexation of national pension is linked to a price index, and the indexation of supplementary pensions since 1996 is linked to two different combined indices, one for disability pensions and another for old-age pensions.

In countries in which the adjustment of pensions is linked with a consumer price index, or with a comparable measure of inflation, and is regularly affected, the real average pension amount could not decrease, but the pensioners relative income could, compared to the active population. The pension adjustment, which is linked to wages, maintains the relative position of retirees. The pensioners can have a share of the growth of productivity. Wage indexation leads to the risk of a reduced real pension if the inflation rate is higher than the growth rate. When productivity rises, wage indexation keeps the required contribution rate constant, while price indexation allows the contribution rate to fall.

Pension adjustments are linked to the trend in the nominal average income, or to the nominal average wage of the active population. The effects of pension adjustments on the real average pension depends on either of these reference factors as distinct from the rise in inflation. If these income or wage movements are on average higher than the average increase in inflation, then any immediate pension adjustment leads to a tendency for average pensions to rise slightly.

Since retirees care about their relative and absolute positions but Governments often wish to use the growth of productivity for other purposes, for example to offset rising dependency rates, the best indexation from both the pensioners and the public expenditures view of point, in an economy with slow age transition, might be the average of a price and a wage index.

Finland has gradually moved from wage to price indexation of earnings-related supplementary pension benefits. The private sector pension scheme that was introduced in 1962 was indexed to wages until 1976. Between 1977 and 1995 it was adjusted to an average of the price and wage index. Due to the economic recession at the beginning of the 1990s the revaluation of pensions was temporarily suspended in 1993 and 1994. In 1996 the weight of the former was increased from 50 to 80 per cent and the weight of the latter was reduced from 50 to 20 per cent.

In this paper I analyse the effects of indexation reform in Finland on old-age pension expenditure, old-age pension benefits, and the income distribution between the old-age retired and the active population. In Finland there is no published analysis of the effects of the reform of the 1996 indexation on expenditure for old-age pension or on old-age pension benefits.

The analysis concerning the macro- and microeconomic effects of indexation on pension expenditure and benefits in Finland are based on the whole pension system, including old-age retirement (60% of pension expenditure), disability pension (25%), other forms of early retirement (6%) and survivors pension (9%). The commissions that analysed hypothetical effects of different reforms used two alternatives: value adjustment either by price index or wage index, and the same index for both the national pension and the supplementary pension, but the reformed pension adjustment is now much more complicated than it was before.

The Finnish Pension Schemes

The Mandatory Pension System

The Finnish mandatory pension system consists of a national flat rate pension and different earnings-related pension schemes (Figure 1).

Figure 1. The Finnish Pension Schemes

	Earnings-related supplementary schemes		
National pension act	Private sector Employee's pension acts	Self-employed's pension acts	Public sector's pension acts
	- Employee's pension act - Temporary employee's pension act - Seamen's pension act - Freelance employee's pension act	- Self-employed's pension act - Farmer's pension act	- State employee's pension act - Local Government employees' pension act - Evangelic-Lutheran church's pension act

Before the reforms in the 1990s, the Finnish National Pension Act from 1939 was totally revised in the mid-1950s. The present national pension act came into effect in 1957. The public sector pension schemes were reformed in the mid-1960s. The first mandatory earnings-related private sector pension scheme was introduced at the end of the 1950s. In the early 1970s the supplementary pension system was expanded to cover self-employed and farmers, and the benefit level increased. In the 1980s new pension forms were introduced, i.e. access to early old-age pension and early disability pension.

The proportion of pensioners in Finland receiving a supplementary pension, in addition to the national pension, was 40 per cent in 1970, 50 per cent in 1980 and 80 per cent in 1990.

Figure 2. Integrating the National Pension and the Earnings-related Pensions to Total Pension

a) Between 1957 and 1995.   b) Since 1997

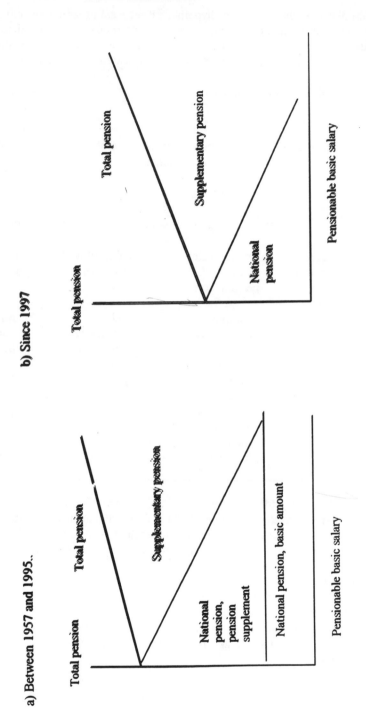

The national pension's share of total old age pensions among the Finnish elderly was 29 per cent in 1995, compared with 76 per cent 1965, 57 per cent 1975 and 46 per cent in 1985. Because the national pension act was reformed in 1996 to be gradually pension income tested, its share of total pension is continuing to diminish (Figure 2).

The Economic Position of Pensioners

The importance of earnings-related statutory pension schemes for the income package of the Finnish elderly is growing while the relative importance of the national pension is falling (figure 3), because the pension scheme of the private sector will not reach maturity before the beginning of the 21st century.

The average real total income among the Finnish elderly has grown by 120 per cent between 1966 and 1990. An interesting effect of the improvements in statutory pension benefits on behaviour in old age is that the relative importance of factor income (work income, self employment and capital income) has decreased from about 70 to 7 per cent (Figure 3).

The pensioners receiving national pension benefits are entitled to tax reductions. A retired person without other income than benefits from the national pension scheme does not pay income tax. That is why the Finnish national pension benefits in figure 4 are related to the average industrial net wage.

In 1950, the national pension was 10 per cent of the average industrial net wage, in 1960 32 per cent, in 1970 40 per cent, and in 1975 about 50 per cent. After 1975 the replacement rate of the national pension has declined and it was about 40 per cent in 1990, despite the reform of national pension benefits in the early 1980s. The rise of real income was high during the 1980s, on average about 4 per cent per year.

The net replacement rate of the public sector pension has been about 70 per cent of previous wage since 1950. Most of the private sector pension schemes were introduced in the beginning of the 1960s. The net replacement rate has risen from about 40 to about 60 per cent between 1965 and 1990.

In Finland the average real total pension increased significantly, by 136 per cent from 1970 to 1989. The average real national pension increased by only 38 per cent. The large take-up of the income-related supplementary pensions played a substantial part in the rise of the average real pension. The primary reason for the increase in the pension benefits lies in the development of the supplementary pension schemes.

Figure 3. The Development of the Average Annual Income among Finnish Elderly, 1966-1990(FIM, in 1990 Prices) (source: Jäntti et al 1996)

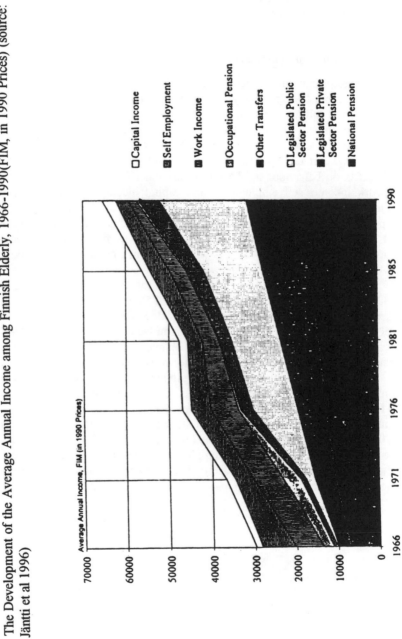

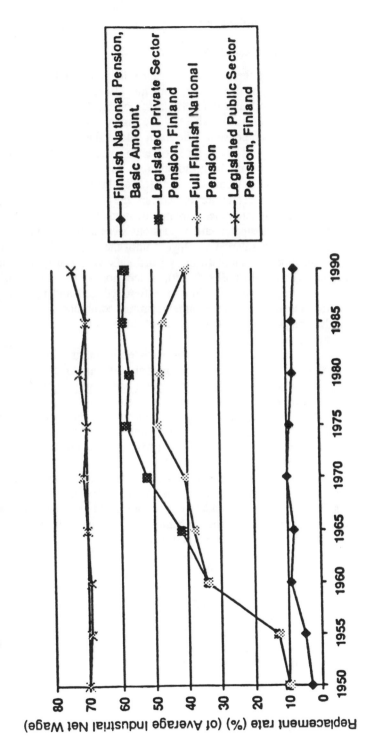

Figure 4. Finnish National Pension as a Percent of Average Industrial Net Wage and Net Replacement Rates (Pension/Previous Wage, %) in the Finnish Legislated Supplementary Pensions, 1950-1990 (Jantti et al 1996)

The Indexation of Finnish Pensions

Changes in Pension Adjustment Rules

In Finland the benefits of the national pension scheme are linked to the consumer price index since the present pension act came into effect in 1957. The main purpose of the national pension scheme is to eliminate poverty (politically defined) in the country. It does not automatically share in the growth of wages but maintains the purchasing power of basic pension. The main rule is that the pension benefits are increased at the beginning of each year in order to correspond to the rise in the cost of living. During periods of high inflation in the 1970s and the 1980s, the revaluation of the national pension was made two or three times a year. After a three year period of negative economic growth in the beginning of the 1990s the Government decided to ignore indexation provision in 1993 and 1994.

The earnings-related supplementary pensions were adjusted in accordance with a general wage index for salaried employees until the end of 1976. Between 1977 and 1995 the adjustment of supplementary pensions was linked to the average price and wage index (here called EPI 50:50), except for 1993 and 1994, when the indexation of earnings-related pensions was first reduced and then stopped. The impact of both price and wage developments on this combined index was fifty-fifty. This means that the pension adjustments have lead to an increase in the real average pension and in real pension costs.

Until the end of 1992, the Finnish legislated earnings-related pensions were totally financed by the employer's contribution. An employee's contribution (at present 3%) was introduced in 1993. This reform had an impact on the indexation of pensionable basic salary and pension benefits. Instead of a gross wage index, a net wage index (wage index minus employee's contribution) has been used in pension adjustment since 1993. In practice the reform contributes to lower pension benefits and lower pension costs in the future, and it has an effect on the relative economic position of the retired population.

Indexation was an issue in Finnish pension reform in the middle of the 1990s. The national pension is at present linked to the consumer price index. A new combined index for value adjustment of the running old age pension benefits to all the legislated supplementary pension schemes was introduced from the beginning of 1996, in addition to the existing combined index.

Since 1996 two different indices are used for benefits from the Finnish supplementary pension schemes: the "old" index EPI 50:50 (average of net wage and price index) is used to adjust the pensionable wage, to calculate the starting pension benefit and to adjust disability pension and other pensions before the age for old-age retirement (65 years).

In the case of early retirement (under 65 years) the pension is adjusted with the EPI 50:50 index. Early retirement is extremely common in Finland; only 11 per cent of present age cohorts continue working until they reach 65 years of age.

Figure 5. Indexation of Pensionable Income and Supplementary Old-Age Pensions in Finland Before and After 1996

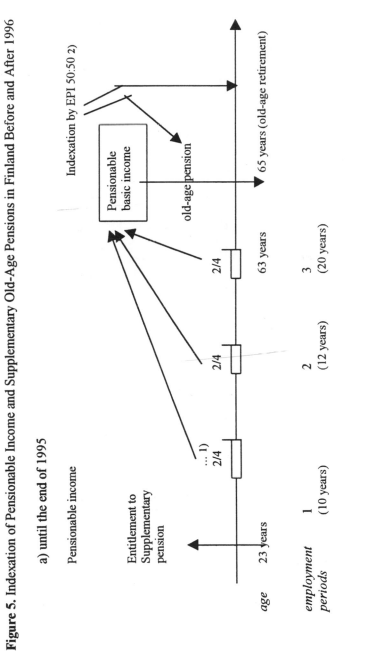

a) until the end of 1995

Pensionable income

Indexation by EPI 50:50 2)

Pensionable basic income

old-age pension

Entitlement to Supplementary pension

...1)
2/4

2/4

2/4

65 years (old-age retirement)

63 years

age   23 years

employment   1   2   3
periods   (10 years)   (12 years)   (20 years)

1)   2 average income years of the 4 last years
2)   average of wage and consumer price index

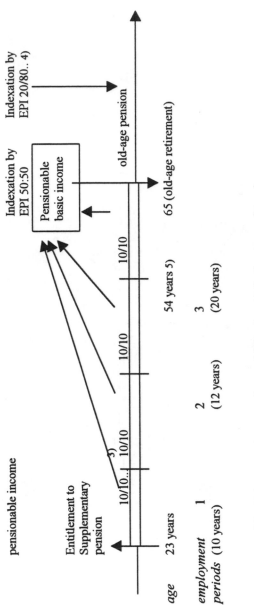

b) since 1996

pensionable income

Indexation by EPI 20/80.. 4)

Indexation by EPI 50:50

Pensionable basic income

old-age pension

Entitlement to Supplementary pension

10/10... 10/10   10/10   10/10
        3)

age   23 years

employment   1   2   3
periods   (10 years)   (12 years)   (20 years)

                                      54 years 5)

                                   65 (old-age retirement)

3)   average of the 10 last years income minus employee´s contribution to pension scheme
4)   20 % of wage index minus employee´s contribution and 80% of consumer price index
5)   actuarial interruption

The "new" index (in this paper called EPI 20:80), that was introduced as a part of the recent pension reforms, counts 20 per cent of the changes in net wage index and 80 per cent of the changes in the consumer price index. It is only used for value adjustment of running old-age pension benefits among the population 65 years of age and over. The "old" EPI 50:50 index is also at present used in the revaluation of the pensionable basic salary and the amount of the starting pension in the case of retirement at the age of 65 (Figure 5).

The method for calculating pensionable basic income was also reformed. Instead of two of the last four years income per employment period, average income during the ten last years per employment period contributes to pensionable basic income (Figure 5).

Theoretical Aspects of Indexation Reform

The Finnish reform of indexation only deals with payable old-age benefits from the earnings-related supplementary pension schemes. The impact of real wage growth on the old-age pension is decreased by the reform.

The "old" employee's pension index (EPI 50:50) was increasing payable pension benefits by 50 per cent of real wage growth in every year. If the growth of the real wage was 1.5 per cent per year (the growth of productivity about 3%), real growth of the supplementary pension was 0.75 per cent per year. In 14 years (present life expectancy for Finnish men at the age of 65) and 18 years (life expectancy for Finnish women at the age of 65) the real pension would have risen by 10.5 and 13.5 per cent respectively.

With the present indexation (EPI 20:80) old-age pensioners share only 20 per cent of real wage growth (Figure 6). The real pension rises by 0.3 per cent if the growth of real wage is 1.5 per cent. In 14 respective 18 years the real pension would rise by 4.2 and 5.2 per cent respectively.

The effects of reformed indexation on pension benefits in old age, old-age pension expenditure, and the hypothetical contribution rate to a PAYG-system (old-age pension expenditure/gross salary in the economy), depend on economic growth and inflation. Real productivity growth is necessary for real wage growth.

Figure 6. Real Change in Pension Index at Different Real Wage Growth Levels

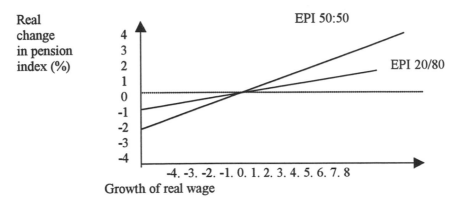

After the indexation reform, the effect that the real growth of wages in the economy has on the real growth of old age pension benefits is smaller. The faster the real growth of wages is, the more old-age pensioners loose, compared to before this indexation. On the other hand, the more negative the real growth of wages is, the more old-age pensioners win. Even high inflation makes it possible for the old-age pensioners to take advantage of the reform (Figure 7).

Figure 7. Real Change in Pension Index at Different Inflation Levels (real Wage Growth = 0)

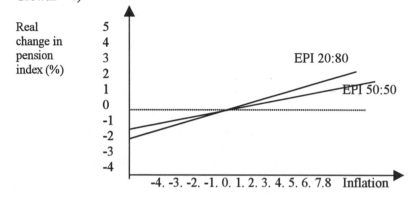

From the macroeconomic point of view, the consequences of the reform of indexation are quite the opposite: during periods of fast economic growth that make large real growth of wages possible, pension expenditure will fall relative to the gross income of the economy. And during periods of slow or negative real growth, when savings are most needed, pension expenditure will rise.

The ideal development of the economy, both before and after the reform of the indexation of old-age supplementary pension, is high real economic growth. It will decrease relative pension expenditure and increase real pension benefits. The impact of reformed indexation is that during economic growth the relative decrease of old-age pension expenditure in the economy is bigger than the increase of real pension income received by the elderly.

Demographic and Economic Factors that Affect Pensions

Pension Expenditure

During 1980-1992, real expenditure on earnings-related pensions, including all forms of pension, increased by an average of 7 per cent per year. The main reason for the increased cost was the increase in the amount of retired persons (60%) (Ministry of Finance 1994).

The impact of indexation on the real growth of pension expenditure 1980-1992 was 20% (Figure 8) and that of the benefit level connected to the maturing of supplementary pension schemes 20 %.

Figure 8. The Real Increase of the Expenditure of Earnings-related Pensions and the Effect of Indexation (EPI 50:50) on the Real Pension Expenditure in Finland (Ministry of Finance 1994)

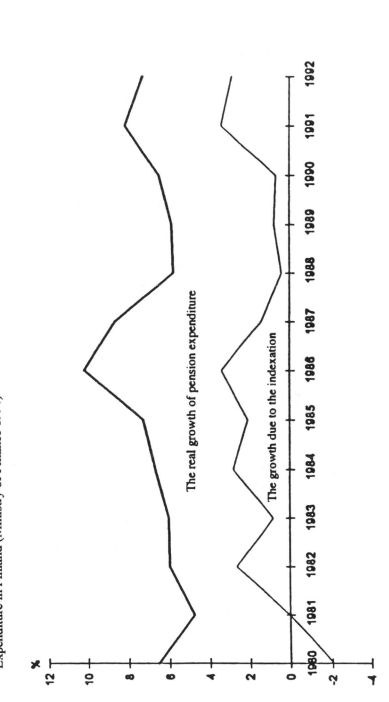

Age Transition

The main demographic factors contributing to the increase of pension expenditure are changes in age composition (proportion of the population aged 65 or over), the old-age dependency ratio, labour force participation ratio, economic dependency ratio, and life expectancy.

Between 1980 and 1994.the number of people in Finland aged 65 years or over increased by 25 per cent, from 12 to 14 per cent of the total population (in absolute numbers from 580,000 to 720,000). The average growth of the aged population was 1.7 % per year. The age transition in Finland is very fast, and will continue to be so, especially at the beginning of the next century. Old-age dependency ratio (population aged 65 years and over/population of working age) will increase dramatically, by 100 per cent between 1990 and 2030. In 1990 there were 19 and in 2030 there will be 39 old age retired people, aged 65 and over, per 100 persons 15-64 years of age. Only three other EU-countries have a faster demographic transition than Finland. The old-age dependency ratio is the most common theoretical measure for the financing burden in a PAYG-system, as the Finnish supplementary pension systems mostly are (the share of funds in the Employee's Pension Act is about 20%).

Dependency levels are generally underestimated when calculated solely on an age basis. Economic dependency ratio (population aged 65 years or over/actually working population) is a more sensitive measure of the economic impact on population ageing, and on the financing burden in a PAYG-financed pension system, than is an old-age dependency ratio. The level of labour force participation of the population of working age is changing. The rate of early retirement and unemployment, the length of full-time education and the female labour market behaviour all affect the real economic dependency ratio.

Economic dependency in a Nordic context is not dependency of the family but the state. Periods of high unemployment can, for example, decrease the number of actually working population. In Finland, most women work outside their homes. On the other hand, early retirement before the age of 65 is very common. Due to the high unemployment rate in the 1990s, the relative and the absolute number of active population has decreased (Figure 9). The economic dependency ratio is thus much higher than old age dependency ratio.

The indexation of pensions does not react to the changing level of unemployment and labour market participation. A high level of unemployment has effects on the gross income and distribution in the economy. The unemployed do not contribute to the supplementary pension schemes, the real pension grows if there is real wage growth, and finally, the active population's contribution to the pension system is rising.

At the age of 65, the present average life-expectancy in Finland is about 16 years (14 years for men and 18 years for women). In the beginning of the 21st century it is estimated to be about 17 years which is 5 years more than in 1950 (Table 1).

Figure 9. Economic Dependency Ratio in Finland, 1980- 2030 (Ministry of Social Welfare and Health 1994)

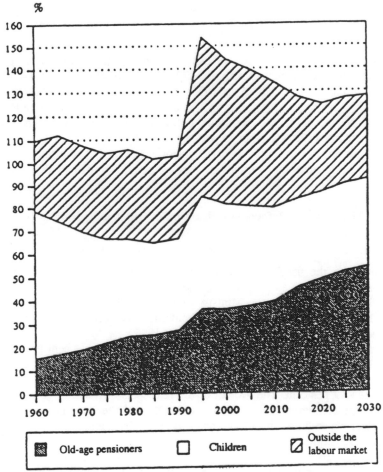

Table 1. The Average Life-Expectancy at the Age of 65 for Men and Women in Finland

Year	Men	Women	Difference Women-Men
1950	10.8	13.9	3.1
1960	11.3	13.6	2.3
1970	11.4	14.5	3.1
1980	12.5	16.8	4.3
1990	13.9	18.0	4.1
2000	14.9	18.6	3.7
2010	15.4	18.8	3.4

Source: Ministry of Health and Social Affairs (1994)

Between 1980 and 1995 the increase of the average life expectancy in old age was 12 per cent and the increase of the absolute number of population, aged 65 years or over, was 25 per cent.

Economic Factors

Economic growth is the most central factor relating to the financing of pension expenditure. The average real growth of GDP per year in Finland was 4.4% in the 1950s, 5 % in the 1960s, 3.9 % in the 1970s, 3.6% in the 1980s and -3.2% between 1990 and 1993. At present the real growth is about 4 % per year but there is a long way up to the level of the last four decades (see Figure 10). The present unemployment rate (1997) is about 15 per cent.

The major reforms of supplementary pension schemes that contributed to better benefits can be located after periods of high economic growth in the 1970s and 1980s.

Economic Effects of the Reformed Indexation of Old Age Pension

An Outlook

In opposition to the usual way of analysing the effects of reform, I base my calculations on retroactive data for the period 1980-1995. The material consists of the data files constructed by the Ministry of Social Affairs and Health of Finland (1995). The question is: what would developments have been like if the indexation reform had been introduced in 1980 instead of in 1996.

In the 1980s the real growth of GDP was an average 4.1 per cent per year, and the growth of wages and salaries was 3.9 per cent. During the first five years of the 1990s, the average real growth of GDP was -1.4 per cent and that of wages and salaries was -2.9 per cent. The growth of the real costs of the old age pension has been very fast compared to the growth of GDP and the amount of wages and salaries. Real expenditure on old age pensions grew by about 6 per cent per year during 1980-95 (Figure 11).

Due to the very high unemployment rate in Finland in the 1990s, productivity (real GDP/active population) and the real amount of wages and salaries/active population have grown more than GDP and the total amount of wages and salaries, especially at the beginning of the 1990s. Old age pension benefits per old age pensioner were showing a very rapid real growth, compared to the economic indices (Figure 12).

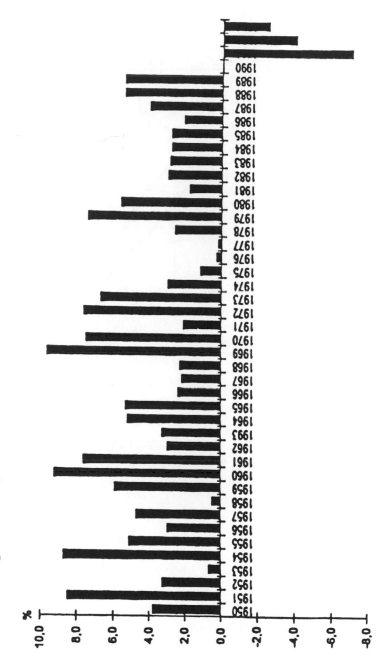

Figure 10. Real growth of GDP in Finland, 1950-1994 (Ministry of Finance 1994)

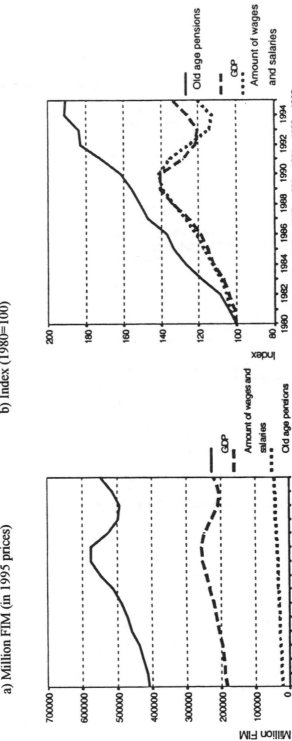

Figure 11. GDP, Amount of Wages and Salaries and Expenditure for Old Age Pensions in Finland, 1980-95

a) Million FIM (in 1995 prices)   b) Index (1980=100)

Figure 12. GDP/Active Population, Amount of Wages and Salaries/Active Population and Expenditure for Old Age Pensions/Pensioner in Finland, 1980-95

a) Million FIM (in 1995 prices)....   b) Index (1980=100)

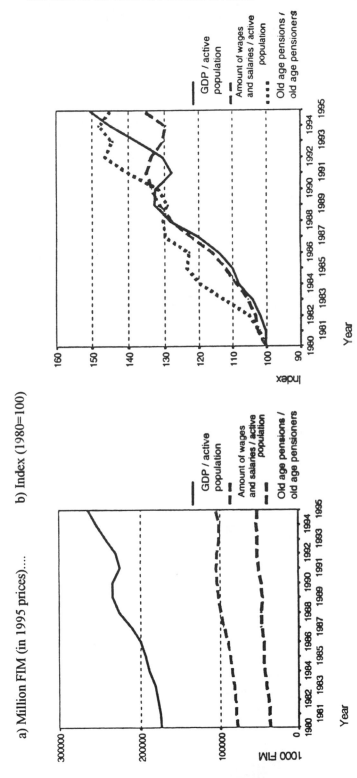

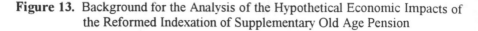

Figure 13. Background for the Analysis of the Hypothetical Economic Impacts of
the Reformed Indexation of Supplementary Old Age Pension

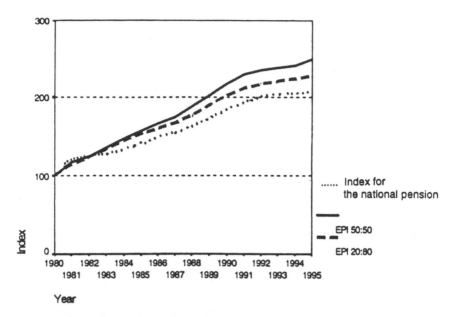

Figure 13 illustrates the differences between the "old" index (EPI 50:50) for
adjustment of supplementary old-age pension and the "new" one (EPI 20:80). In
1995 the "new" index for supplementary old age pension is 8.6 per cent lower than
the "old" index. These indices make the background for my retroactive analysis of
the hypothetical microeconomic and macroeconomic effects of the indexation
reform, under the assumption that the "new" index EPI 20:80 that came into effect
in 1996, would have come into effect in 1980. The indexation reform did not cover
benefits from the national pension scheme which at present are adjusted by the
consumer price index.

Microeconomic Effects of the Reformed Indexation of Old-Age Pension

It is important to notice that the Finnish reform of the indexation of pension
concerns only the revaluation of payable old-age supplementary pension. The
analysis, made before the reform in 1996, concerning microeconomic effects of
different hypothetical reforms of all forms of pension, can only be used on old-age
pension benefits but not on macroeconomic effects on the role of pension
expenditure in the Finnish economy.

The Commission of Social Expenditure (Ministry of Social Affairs and Health
1994) has calculated the effects of different forms of indexation on the
supplementary pension, including disability and survivors pensions, by comparing a
supplementary pension index EPI 50:50 to the index EPI 20:80 on the development
of the old-age pension using different assumptions about productivity growth
(Table 2).

Table 2. The Effect of the Reform of Pension Adjustment on the Real Old-Age Pension during Different Productivity Growth in Finland

Pension Lasted Years	Low Growth (1%)	Medium Growth (1,5%)	High Growth (2%)
10	-2.4	-4.2	-7.8
20	-5.4	-7.8	-10.2
30	-7.8	-11.4	-14.4
40	-10.2	-14.4	-18.2

The reduction of the pension adjustment link with the wage index from 50 to 20 per cent means that a Finnish man who retires in 1997 at the age of 65 looses between 4 and 9 per cent during retirement (14 years on average), depending on economic growth in Finland. A Finnish woman with a life expectancy of 18 years at the age of 65 will get about 5 to 10 per cent less in her last pension due to the indexation reform.

I have analysed the hypothetical effects of the reformed indexation using the retroactive material from the period 1980-1995 (Figure 14).

If the new index for supplementary pension had been introduced in 1980, a Finnish man of 65 years of age, who retired that year and who then had a life expectancy of 12 years, would have lost about 5.1 per cent in pension benefits, compared with the actual old index. A Finnish woman with a life expectancy of 17 years at the age of 65 would have lost about 7 per cent because of the reform of indexation.

Macroeconomic Effects of the Reformed Indexation

The material for my retroactive analysis of the hypothetical macroeconomic effects of index reform also consists of the data base produced by Ministry of Health and Social Affairs of Finland (1995).

If the new index for supplementary pensions had been introduced in 1980, the total real expenditure for old age pension in 1995 would have been 6.2 per cent less compared to the actual costs when using the old indexation (Figure 15).

Between 1980 and 1995 old-age pension expenditure has grown from 5.4 to 7.6 per cent of GDP, an increase of 41 per cent. The growth is only due to supplementary pension expenditure. If the present index EPA 20:80 had been introduced in 1980, total old-age pension expenditure as percentage of GDP in 1995 would have been 7.2 per cent and would have grown by 33 per cent during the period (Figure 16).

Figure 14. Old Age Pension/Pensioner in Finland Using the Old Index for Supplementary Pension EPI 50:50 and, Hypothetically, using the New Index EPI 20:80, 1980-95.

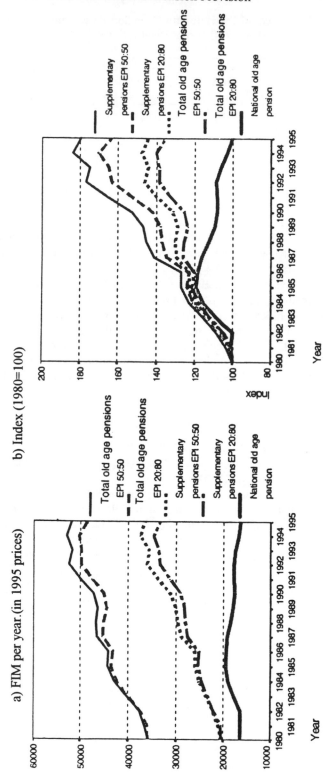
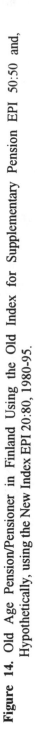

a) FIM per year.(in 1995 prices)

b) Index (1980=100)

Figure 15. Old-Age Pension Expenditure, 1980-95, and Hypothetical Old-Age Pension Using the New Index for Supplementary Pension

a) Million FIM.(in 1995 prices)..... b) Index (1980=100)

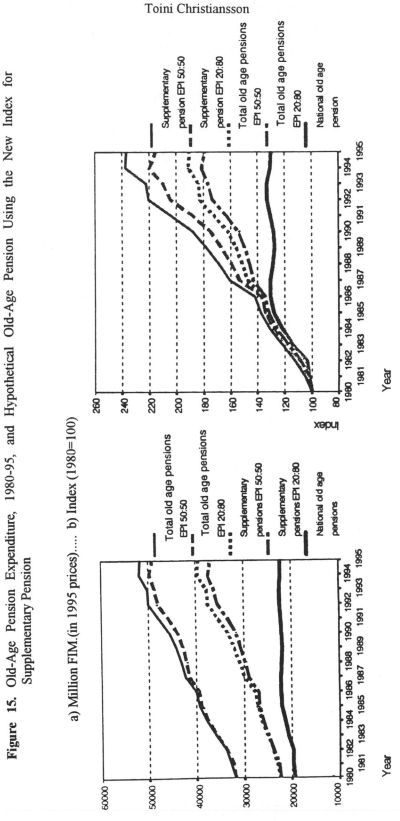

Figure 16. Expenditure for Old Age Pension as Percentage of GDP in Finland, 1980-95, and Hypothetical Expenditure under the New Index for Supplementary Pension.

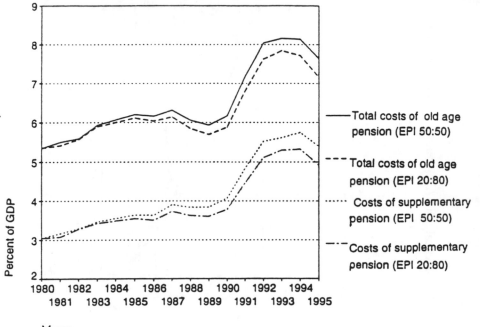

Costs of old age pensions as percentage of GDP (%)

According to the Commission of Social Expenditure (Ministry of Health and Social Affairs 1994), the indexation reform would decrease the total supplementary pension expenditure, in relation to the amount of wages and salaries, by 0.8 to 1.6 per cent in 35 years, depending on productivity growth. Because of the fact that old-age pension expenditure amounts to only 60 per cent of total pension expenditure in Finland, the impact is smaller than the one calculated.

As a percentage of wages and salaries in Finland, old-age pension expenditure has grown from 12.1 to 19.1 per cent, or by 58 per cent between 1980 and 1995. If the index EPI 20:80 had been introduced in 1980, the growth would have been 48 per cent, from 12.1 to 17.9 (Figure 17).

Figure 17. Expenditure for Old Age Pension in Finland as Percentage of the Amount of Wages and Salaries, 1980-95

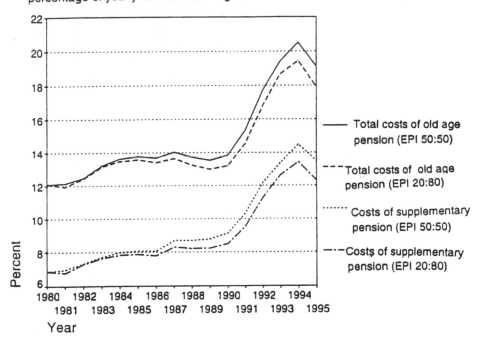

Total costs of Old age- and Supplementary pensions as percentage of yearly salaries and wages

Conclusion

The conclusion regarding the economic impact of the Finnish reform of the indexation of old-age supplementary pension is, that the higher economic growth is and the greater the relative savings of old age pension expenditure in the economy are, the more pension income as a percentage of wages decreases and the more the difference in purchasing power grows between the active population and pensioners.

Theoretically, a change from wage towards price indexation of pensions, as with the Finnish reform, reduces the rate of growth of pension expenditure temporarily, until all employees have retired after the change. Afterwards, expenditure growth resumes the pattern it would have had without the change.

The main purpose of supplementary pension schemes is to ensure that people in old age are guaranteed a level of living related to their level of living they had when they were working. If this purpose means a guaranteed absolute level of living and maintained purchasing power within the retired generation, the pension should only be linked with a price index. Under price indexation the pensioner cannot gain from real economic growth in the country. Hence, the relative position of a pensioner, compared to the level of living among the active population, will get worse.

If the purpose of supplementary pension schemes are defined to maintain the relative economic position of pensioners by raising their pension income as fast as the real wage grows, the pension adjustment should be linked with a wage index. In countries with public pension policy this choice is a political one.

In Finland the adjustment of the national pension is linked with the consumer price index. If the pension adjustment is regularly affected, the real average national pension can not get smaller, but the pensioners relative income, compared to the active population, falls because the national pension does not react to the growth of productivity and wages.

The present adjustment of supplementary old-age pensions is linked to the consumer price index by 80 per cent and to the wage index by 20 per cent. The real average supplementary old-age pension can fall slightly if there is no real wage growth in the economy. The present combined index does not maintain the relative position of old-age pensioners as well as the earlier index. Before this indexation the old-age pensioners entitled to supplementary pension could share 50 per cent of the real growth of wages. The present indexation redistributes 20 per cent of the real growth of wages.

The aim for the Finnish pension reform was to decrease pension expenditure and the contribution rate. The present indexation which is more strongly linked to prices than to wages, allows the contribution rate to fall by the relative fall of pension expenditure when productivity and wages are rising. It has an impact on income distribution between the elderly and the active population. The old-age pensioners relative economic position will be weakened. The rate of weakening of the old-age pensioners relative purchasing power is related to real economic growth.

References

Franco D, Munzi T. *Public Pension Expenditure Prospects in the European Union: A Survey of National Projections.* European Commission, Directorate General II, Economic and Financial Affairs, 1996.

International Social Security Association. *The impact of changing life expectancy and retirement patterns on pension costs.* Geneva, 1992.

Jäntti M, Kangas O, Ritakallio VM. "From Marginalism to Institutionalism: Distributional Consequences of the Transformation of the Finnish Pension Regime." *Review of Income and Wealth,* 1996;42:4.

Ministry of Finance. *Suomen eläkejärjestelmän rahoituksen kestävyys, oikeudenmukaisuus ja taloudelliset kannustimet. Valtiovarainministeriön työryhmämuistioita,* 1994:7. Helsinki:Valtiovarainministeriö, 1994.

Ministry of Health and Social Affairs. *Betänkande av pensionskommittén 1990.* Kommittébetänkande 1991:41. Helsingfors: Statens tryckericentral, 1991.

Ministry of Health and Social Affairs. *Betänkande av socialutgiftskommissionen.* Kommittébetänkande 1994:9. Helsingfors: Statens tryckericentral, 1994.

Ministry of Health and Social Affairs. Data file on expenditure for social security. 1995.

Pusa O. *Ideal of an earnings-related pension scheme and the earnings-related pension scheme in Finland.* Kuopio: Kuopio University Publications, 1994.

World Bank. *Averting the Old Age Crisis.* New York: Oxford University Press, 1994.

13 U.S. SOCIAL SECURITY REFORM AND INTERGENERATIONAL EQUITY

Teresa Ghilarducci

"Reptiles and badly frightened people have two characteristics in common: they have no sense of humor and they eat their young (Schnarch, p. 136)"

Do the Old Eat the Young?

One of the persistent allegations against the U.S. Social Security system comes from both ends of the political spectrum, the right and the left. Feminist economists argue Social Security benefits men by tracing its patriarchal roots. The program was based on a model of a male breadwinner with dependent women and children and the original act excluded industries with high concentrations of female employment. Indeed, twenty percent of single American older women are poor (though Social Security halved that rate from 1971 to 1991) while child poverty remains at the shocking rate of 20%. Old women living alone in the U.K. and Australia have even higher poverty rates than the U.S., over 60% and 40% respectively. In the U.S. older men's poverty is just 8% – higher than international standards – but lower than male workers. The World Bank report emphasizes that this is not unusual: the elderly are often better off than workers and their children in most OECD nations (World Bank, 1994, 77).

Evidence to support the old-eat-the-young hypothesis includes the observation that younger cohorts earn a lower rate of return because of the mechanics of a maturing system. In most cases, when existing pay-as-you go systems began, many workers paid for a few retirees and the ratio of beneficiaries to workers was very low. As the systems mature, longevity increases, more workers retire, and the ratio rises. Workers paying taxes at the time the ratio is high tend to have higher tax rates, thus making transfers to generations that are currently receiving benefits (World Bank, 1994 and Chen and Goss, 1997). National systems are at various stages of maturity and some are nearly complete in their maturation. Chen and Goss surveyed the research on rates of return and found a consensus that earlier cohorts have higher average returns to their contributions. One study estimated that individuals retiring from 1960 and 1968 (those who started work at about the inception of the U.S. system) received a 12.5% return while individuals who are twenty years younger received a 5.9% return. Though this violates strict horizontal equity – a payroll dollar invested in the same program does not get the same return – the public policy intent is not to deliberately favor a privileged and powerful group. The good intentions of public policy are not so apparent when a society moves somewhat successfully to halve the rate of poverty among one generation while tolerating persistently high levels of child poverty.

141

The form of pension indexation also affects intergenerational equity. The U.S., Canada and the United Kingdom index pensions to prices in order to maintain absolute levels of pension adequacy. However, this feature has poignant political consequences when real wages growth is negative. In the 1980s and early 1990s, U.S. Social Security pensions grew faster than wages – this violated a sense of fairness and old people were seen as not sharing in economic decline – or rather in the decline in worker's bargaining power. Austria and Mexico index pensions to wages and Japan and Germany index pensions to net-of-taxes wages, so pensioners bear the brunt of a rising tax burden. Wage indexation – in absence of price inflation – means that the elderly share in the productivity gains of the current generation. A nation may want to spend productivity gains in ways other than keeping the elderly at the same relative position. Switzerland compromises and uses a fifty-fifty combination of wage and price growth to index pensions. A 1983 Canadian recommendation to switch to wage indexation so that the seniors are not "immune to the vicissitudes of economic growth" is being considered in Sweden (Wolfson and Murphy, 1996, 94). Sweden is also indexing pensions by average longevity, so that the elderly will stay in the same relative position as the definition of who is old becomes more strict.

Furthermore, the World Bank report emphasizes that even if the pay-go-system has no overt intent to shift resources away from the young, the drag on economic growth (these systems cause) lowers future economic growth. Therefore the effect of public pension systems on economic growth and savings is an intergenerational equity issue.

Regression Analysis

This paper aims to be an initial step in a larger research project on intergenerational equity issues in public retirement systems. One way to assess these arguments is to test the hypothesis that a nation's pension effort (defined as the amount of GDP spent on pensions for every person over 65) is enhanced when the amount of money spent on children (proxied here as education spending per GDP per young person) is reduced.

I call this "the old-eat-the-young hypothesis." In the literature it is generally called the pluralist hypothesis (Pampel and Williamson, 1994). The model states that social spending is determined by political interest groups competing for particular programs that benefit each group. Public choice theory complements the pluralist hypothesis which is that all politicians are vote getters so they act to elicit the support of (World Bank, 1994) or quell the discontent of a voting block that is active and vocal – the gray lobby (Pierson, 1996) Class coalitions are less important in explaining social spending in societies when workers are divided and splintered by ethnic, regional, and other interests.

Another political science model – "industrialism" – explaining social welfare development argues that, as nations industrialize, pension spending increases because as kinship networks are weakening the affordability of Government-based social insurance grows. As nations become richer, adults want to live independently from their adult children. These pull and push factors elicit public spending on the old and young. The industrialism hypothesis would expect the finding that pensions and education spending grow together and interpret it as a spurious correlation. The real cause of both increasing is GDP growth and the achievement of a high degree of urbanization and industrial work.

Another dominant theory of social welfare development are the class-based theories. One variant – the social democratic hypothesis – argues that under industrial conditions workers use market power and solidarity to maximize income, leisure, and obtain protection from being too old, poor, or young to work. The neo-Marxist variant is that capitalists use social welfare programs to quell serious labor revolt. Both class-based theories would be supported by an empirical finding that education and pension spending grow together (Pampel and Williamson, 1994).

I include the feminist hypothesis, which is a variant of the pluralist hypothesis. The feminist model explains that coalitions are formed across particular interest groups. Since patriarchal interests are the most powerful the feminist hypothesis predicts that social welfare programs bypass women and, by extension, children's, needs and interest in autonomy in favor of protecting or promoting male interests.

I estimated the following equations (1 and 2) using ordinary least square regression to examine how "pension effort," defined here as Government spending (as a percent of GDP) on pensions per old person, is affected by "education effort" defined as Government spending (as percent of GDP) on education per child, and the expected number of years spent in retirement and the ratio of young people to the old population attempts to capture the relative size of the cohort. The expected years in retirement is the difference between the expected longevity and the mandatory age of retirement years. I used data from 65 countries for the year 1986, the latest year in which comparable data could be found for all 65 nations. Pension effort is the dependent variable.

1. pension effort = β_0 + β_1 education effort + β_2 years of retirement (men) + β_3 ratio of young to old;
2. pension effort = β_0 + β_1 education effort + β_2 years of retirement (women) β_3 ratio or young to old.

The first equation takes into account the number of retirement years for men and the second equation does so for women. Given the pluralist (do-the-old-eat-the-young) hypothesis I expect a negative relationship between pension and education. Additionally, I expect a positive relationship between the expected years spent in retirement and Government spending on pension per old person, simply because the longer the number of years people spend in retirement the more expensive the pension. I also included the ratio of the number of people under 15 to the number over 60 in order to crudely gauge political power. One possibility is that if there are a few old people relative to the young that would give them weaker bargaining power. The regression results are reported in Table 1. The comparison between the expected and actual findings are in Table 2.

Table 1. The Relationship Between Pension and Education Spending in 65 Nations

	Value of Coefficient and "t" values in Parenthesis Retirement for Men	Value of Coefficient and "t" values in Parenthesis Retirement for Women
Intercept	7.44 (5.092)	4.842 (2.152)
Education per GDP per child (under 15)	-.00089 (-.654)	-.00108 (-.821)
Years in retirement	.1933 (1.286)	.2599 (2.082)
Ratio of young to old (under 15/over 60)	-.8029 (-4.415)	-.7039 (-3.841)
Observations	47	47
R squared	.703	.522

Table 2. Expected Signs on OLS Regression Predicting Pension Effort by Hypothesis

Independent Variable	Pluralist "old eat the young"	Feminist - variant of pluralist	Industriali zation	Class-based	Ghilarducci Findings
Education effort	Negative	Negative	Positive but Spurious	Positive	Insignificant
Male Years in Retirement	Both positive	Positive	Positive but Spurious	Both Positive	Insignificant
Female Years in Retirement		Negative			Positive
Size of Young cohort relative to old	Negative	Negative	Insign-ificant	Positive	Negative

Pension effort   = pension spending as a percent of GDP per old population
Education effort = education spending as a percent of GDP per young population

Findings

I find mixed and weak support for the pluralist hypothesis (see Table 1). The major finding is that the coefficient on education effort is insignificant for both regressions. This can be interpreted to mean that the effort spent on pensions does not affect the effort spent on education and does not support the pluralist hypothesis.

The expected years spent in retirement for men is, surprisingly, not significant although it is for women. This may mean that if men live longer the amount spent on pension is not increased, whereas it is if women live longer. Perhaps the existence of very old women tends to make the nation spend more per older person on pensions. At first blush this does not support the feminist critique of pension systems; it claims public pension systems are not responsive to many aspects of women's dire needs.

The coefficient on the ratio of young to old persons is negative and significant. It seems when there are relatively more children, pension spending falls for men and women. The size of the cohort could proxy for the political strength of the cohort. This would suggest that the more political strength children have, the more is taken away from old persons, thus supporting the pluralist hypothesis. However, the relative size of the cohort may be picking up the industrialization effect because developing nations have younger populations and lower pension effort.

Further Research Needed on Better Data

Education spending is an inadequate proxy for the state's support of children. There are many ways Government uses tax revenue to enhance the standard of living for children: housing, food programs, children's health and child care programs, and tax subsidies for families with children. A better measure of spending efforts towards children are needed. Pension effort does not count the enormous proportion of health care expenditures that go to the elderly. Moreover, the cultural differences between nations that determine a commitment to pensions and education may be too complex for all factors to be controlled for in a cross-section study using ordinary least squares estimations.

A time series study of one nation would control for cultural and national-specific factors. A next important step in this project is to create indices of federal and state spending efforts towards children and the elderly to examine how they correlate in the same nation over time. Cohort size would be controlled for in order to evaluate the complementarity or substitutability of programs for each generation.

I also have not taken into account the pension spending that goes to children in terms of dependent benefits and disability payments. More than ten percent of beneficiaries of the U.S. Social Security system are under age 65.

Pampel and Williamson's (1994) comprehensive comparative study illustrates the importance of combining regression analysis with detailed case study. Below, I will examine one nation's debate around Social Security reform. In Pampel and Williamson's work the strength of the labor movement determines the expansion of the welfare state. But as Pierson (1996) argues, the politics of retrenchment are different from the politics of expansion. The labor movement may seek to impede retrenchment by exposing politician's stealth and incremental erosion of benefits. Retrenchments cause fear and fear may erode solidarity. Perhaps like reptiles, the old will eat the young in order to manage scarcity and threats.

A detailed examination of the recent debate after the Social Security Advisory panel released its divided report in 1997 illustrates the extent to which a class-based interest group argued for intergenerational equity. The advocates for retrenchment – privatization of Social Security – appealed to intergenerational equity goals explicitly.

Intergenerational Equity and U.S. Organized Labor's Reform Proposals

In 1996, for the first time, the quadrennial Social Security Advisory Council was seriously split between proposals that will fundamentally alter the system's pay-as-you-go structure and one that maintains the current benefit levels. The Advisory Council is composed of three representatives from business, three from labor, one self-employed representative, and five members from the general public.

Five members proposed to replace the pay-as-you-go system with personal saving accounts (PSAs) managed by individual workers. Six labor and public representatives, backed Council member and former Social Security commissioner Robert Ball's "Maintain Benefits Plans" to raise revenues and trim benefits and partially fund the system through investment in private equities managed by an agency. Council Chair Professor Edward Gramlich, now a member of the Federal Reserve Governors and one other member backed a modified privatized, two-tier plan.

The proposals were made in the context of a predicted shortfall in the Social Security trust fund in 2029. Ball's plan was reminiscent of the compromise reached in 1983 when unexpected high inflation and unemployment caused an immediate predicted shortfall. It was solved by Congress and the President and resulted in an equal divide between tax increases and benefit cuts. Most of the benefit cuts were a gradual raising of the age to 67 at which time workers could collect full benefits. The payroll tax was raised more than necessary to solve the deficit. For the first time, benefits were advance funded – the baby boom generation is partially funding their own retirement by paying more tax then required to keep a pay-as-you-go system solvent.

Although, the 1983 solution was designed to keep the system substantially solvent for the next 75 years, the 1994 actuarial report predicted more shortfall than expected. Half of the shortfall comes from wages unexpectedly not growing at the same rate as productivity; clearly a hardship not experienced by any other generation. The most drastic real wage losses were among younger workers.

The major provisions of the Ball plan are the following:

1) raise payroll taxes by 1.6% (.8 each for employers and workers) in 2045 – impacting workers just born;

2) put up to 40% of the Trust Fund in the stock market by year 2014 (this solves half of the deficit and such a plan is favored by some reformers for the Canadian system (Wolfson, 1997) but this has no particular generational effect;

3) compute benefits over earnings for 38 rather than 35 years (this lowers benefits for current workers); and,

4) bring in Government workers not covered by the system – this has no particular generational effect.

The Ball supporters represent a class, rather than a generationally aligned interest group. The Ball plan would, therefore, be expected to favor progressive distribution of risk and return from capital to labor and to low income from high-income groups. The Ball plan keeps the system's defined benefit structure that permits the distribution between high and low income workers. Social Security replaces 80% of the pre-retirement earnings of a low wage worker and 24% of a high wage worker. However, the Ball plan maintains the tax incidence equally divided between labor and capital. Retirees do not bear the risk of inflation or low-wage growth in this plan. Furthermore, Social Security is a mandatory universal defined benefit plan that complements the riskier retirement income sources from private savings and company retirement plans. Making Social Security a defined contribution plan would tip the balance toward riskier streams of retirement income.

The labor movement would be expected to support Social Security. Union members expect to retire – 79% have workplace pensions compared to 39% of non-union workers – and Social Security supplements these bargained pensions. In addition, the labor movement represents the middle class and Social Security is still a middle class benefit. Middle class retirees, family units with $17,000 - $29,000 (in 1990) of income per year (U.S. Department of Labor, 1992; Reno, 1993) received under 40% of their income from Social Security in 1980. However, because of the erosion in pension benefits and coverage, wealth, and wages, Social Security made up 60% of retirement income to this group by 1990. Though a common description of the sources of retirement income is a three-legged stool – for the middle class the retirement income security system is a pyramid; Social Security is the base, employer pensions is the middle, and individual wealth and savings is the top making up less than 10% (Reno, 1993). Ball's plan to keep the system funded by contributions and financial market returns rather than general revenues means there is no explicit tradeoff between Social Security and poverty programs. However, when the Government bonds need to be sold in 2018 to pay for ongoing benefits there may be a squeeze on general revenues.

Labor concedes that workers born after 1940, will receive a smaller percentage of benefits compared to contributions and that current retirees receive much more than they put into the system. But they challenge the "money's worth criteria" because it misses the insurance value of the universal system – a young worker has up to $250,000 worth of life insurance and a valuable indexation provision. The universality solves private market failures and offers insurance without the price of moral hazard or adverse selection that plagues annuity markets. Also, the system forces employers to pay the bulk of the cost by requiring them to collect payments.

Intergenerational Equity and the Privatizing Proposals

The World Bank proposals are similar to the business-aligned Personal Savings Account and the Gramlich plan in that they propose that pay-as-you-go defined benefit pensions be transformed to advance funded defined contribution structure. Among many other advantages both groups claim that transformation would have the following intergenerational advantages:

1. Advance funded pensions will enhance savings and investment, which will raise the productivity and income to future generations.
2. Generations will get the rate of return of the economy at the time they are retired so they will have an interest in maintaining high rates of return on capital growth. In pay-as-you-go-systems their interests are in raising benefits at the expense of young workers.
3. An individual's financial acumen will determine rate of return not the cohort one belongs to.

Each of these arguments is addressed below.

Social Security and Savings

The World Bank claims that pay-as-you-go schemes lower the savings rate and economic growth (World Bank, 1994, 88). Since workers have a guaranteed source of retirement income, the argument goes, they are less likely to save for retirement. Since public pensions are financed by taxes and not returns on accumulated savings, advocates for diminishing Social Security (Feldstein, 1996) argue that lower savings lowers investment and productivity.

However, in a nation, such as the U.S., where retirement is voluntary, the effect of Social Security on savings could lead to the opposite conclusions. Feldstein (1974) agreed the effect of Social Security on savings was ambiguous. Social Security could create a retirement-savings motive so that it actually increases retirement savings.[1] Feldstein (1974, 1995) estimated these two effects by regressing expenditures on personal income, net worth, profits, and Social Security wealth variables, the positive coefficient on the Social Security wealth variable led him to conclude Social Security decreases aggregate savings. Barro (1978) and Munnell (1974) used Feldstein's basic methodology, included labor force variables, and found small and insignificant effects of Social Security on savings. Darby (1978) used consumption variables and found insignificant effects. The evidence on the role of U.S. Social Security on savings behavior is mixed and therefore there is little support for the argument that Social Security takes away from capital formation and the productivity of future generations. Edwards (1995) international studies found per capita growth to be the most important variable determining savings.

Choosing the Right Cohort: The Inexorable Risks of Being in a Large Cohort

Privatization advocates claim the pay-as-you-go systems are Ponzi schemes. In the U.S., baby boomers will start retiring in 12 years and by 2030 100 workers will support 36 retirees, up from 21 in 1995. Populations are graying in most nations (World Bank 1994). Workers would invest their savings and sell assets when retired. However, just as their demand for financial assets lift stock and bond prices, their sell-off starting in the year 2020 will lower asset values. In the U.S. the de-accumulation period will start at about 2025 (Schieber and Shoven, 1994; Bensmen, 1994). This de-accumulation could cause asset values to fall. The anticipated demand for these surplus assets in 2020-2035 is the young populations of Mexico, Brazil, and China and India. This works if these nations have private pension systems that invest in foreign assets and nations have different demographic profiles (World Bank, 1994).

The Class/Not Generational Effects of Privatization

The privatizing plan from the five business-aligned members of the Advisory Council would cut workers' 6.2% share of the payroll tax to 1.2% and require the remaining 5% to be invested in Personal Savings Accounts (PSA's). A financial services company such as a bank, brokerage house or mutual fund would manage a worker's account and invest it according to the worker's wishes whether it be in U.S. Treasuries or junk bonds. The plan calls for a basic safety net of $360 – $410 per month. *Money* magazine computed benefits under both the Ball and PSA plan for several kinds of families (Tritch, 1996). The simulation assumed salaries grew 5% a year, workers retire at 62 and the PSAs would earn 8% per year. The flat monthly benefit of $413 in 1993 was assumed to increase 5% a year. The cost of the transition is $1.2 trillion because current benefits would have to be paid while revenue is being siphoned off in PSA's. The PSA plan raises payroll tax by 1.52% between 1998 to 2069. Spouses' benefits are cut from 50% of the workers' benefit to 33%. (Current benefits are further cut under the PSA plan by raising the age at which full benefits can be collected to age 69 by 2059 and eliminate retirement before age 65 by 2012 but these were not included in the simulation).

Money finds that only young workers making large salaries, and having no periods of unemployment, obtain a substantially larger pension under PSA's than Social Security. Low wage workers who make poor investments would be the biggest losers. They would have less wages and likely would invest conservatively – thus earnings would be lower than 8%. Administrative costs would further lower the rate of return. PSA assumes that fees will only be 0.3%. However, the average growth fund charges 1.4% of the account for administration. If workers want tailored advice the costs could go higher. The PSA's are not indexed to inflation and they may be depleted before a retiree dies.

U.S. Labor: Class or Generation Advocates

During this period, organized labor's lobbying effort against privatization of Social Security seem to be concerned with redistribution issues between high and low income workers. There was no proposal to increase capital's share or to shift more risk on retirees relative to workers. Intensive study about labor's efforts with regard to women, children and old age issues may give better insight into the role American labor plays. This is beyond the scope of this paper.

In 1994, Richard Trumka, the then United Mine Worker of America president and the only labor representative on the 31 member Bipartisan Commission on Entitlement and Tax Reform, argued against an early privatizing plan. Trumka's proposal opted to tax employers immediately and workers in 2020. He proposed to schedule a one percent increase in the payroll tax in 2020 for each employer and worker – from 12.4% to 14.4%. This would solve half of the projected deficit. The rest of the shortfall would be made up by eliminating the cap on employer contributions – employers pay up to $65,400 of wages (Bipartisan Commission Final report, 1995). Trumka's plan differed from the Ball proposal because employers are taxed more, the increase in the age full benefits can be collected was not accelerated, and there was no reliance on the trust fund being invested in the stock market

Wall Street firms and other money management firms, such as State Street Bank, have funded a $2 million campaign to lobby for a PSA-type change in the U.S. Social Security system. They estimate that the proposal would yield 130 million new accounts, $40 billion in new money to manage and $2 billion in fees (in a three year period) (Dreyfuss, 1996). Political support for Social Security in the U.S. may depend on labor's ability to turn the debate from generational conflict to one of conflict between powerful industry interests and the majority of workers.

Conclusions

Neoclassical economics and the promoters of the privatizing model argue that private capital markets are fairer to younger generations because pluralist politics are such that the older generations will always be stronger politically than children. Preliminary regression analysis does not show a noticeable transfer.

The privatization advocates also argue that accumulated assets in the private sector have the best chance of increasing capital formation which helps the future workers, and current pay-as-you-go systems do not provide competitive rates of return for younger generations.

Under a private personal account a retiree's pension depends on the stock market and not the growth in wage income. However, in equilibrium, the returns to capital or the returns to labor can not exceed the growth rate of the economy without the other losing. If the capital market consistently outperforms the rest of the economy it represents a transfer from workers to capital. Privatized, individual-based pensions could divide the interests of the working class – some young people will win, others will lose. Privatized individual pensions may also exaggerate the risks of being in a large cohort – asset value will fall when a large cohort starts to sell. Cohort size problems are not avoided in a privatized model.

A close examination of the current U.S. Social Security debate illustrates that the labor movement has had mixed concerns. The labor-aligned faction of the Advisory Council illustrated more concern for redistribution within the working class rather than concern about generational equity issues or class redistribution. The labor representative on an earlier panel proposed more redistribution within class.

Fundamentally, how societies decide to care for non-earners, whether there is a fixed proportion of output allocated to care for them or it expands with economic growth, or by a realignment of political interests, are partially exhibited by the systems that support the old.

Notes

1. When Social Security passed in 1935 the insurance industry argued that the new system would cause people to stop buying annuities. A year later when friendly Senators asked the industry representatives whether the insurance companies wanted legislation to make Social Security voluntary, the industry said no. The insurance industry was thrilled with the new system. People began to plan for retirement and use the industry products. Furthermore, in the post WW2 period, advance funded private pensions emerged as a key union bargaining issue, in part, because Social Security provided a floor of retirement income and elicited retirement plans among workers. (Ghilarducci, 1992).

In addition, a direct survey of workers (Farkas, 1995) found that 34% of people claim they do not save because of low earnings; 37% do not save because they underestimate what they need in retirement. The rest are split between those who plan their future and save and those who figure they will work until they die. People did not report they lowered their savings because they thought Social Security would provide enough in retirement. Moreover, consumer debt is at all time high when fears over Social Security's solvency is high (Singletary and Crenshaw, 1996.)

References

Barro, Robert J. "Social Security and Private Saving: Another Look: Comment", *Social Security Bulletin*, Vol. 42, No. 5, pp. 33-5, May 1979.

Bensman, Miriam. "The Baby Boomer Boomerang." *Institutional Investor.* September , 53-56, 1994.

Banting, Keith G. and Boadway, Robin, editors. *Reform of the Retirement Income Policy: In International and Canadian Perspectives*, School of Policy Studies, Queen's College, Kingston, Ontario, 1996.

Bergmann, Barbara. *The Economic Emergence of Women* New York, Basic Books, 1986.

Bipartisan Commission on Entitlement and Tax Reform Final Report, Washington DC.: Government Printing Office, 1994.

Chen, Yung-Ping and Stephen Goss, "Are Returns On Payroll Taxes Fair?" in Kingson and Schultz editors. 76 - 90.

Darby, Michael.. "The Effect of Social Security on Income and the Capital Stock." Washington, D.C. American Enterprise Institute for Public Policy Research, 1979.

Dreyfuss, Richard. "The End of Social Security as We Know It?". *Mother Jones*, Nov./Dec. 1996.

Edwards, Sebastian. "Why are Savings Rates so Different across Countries?: An International Comparative Analysis." National Bureau of Economic Research Working Paper 5097, Cambridge Massachusetts, NBER April 1995.

Kostelritz, Julie. "Touching the Rail" *National Journal* . December 23, 1995.

Farkas, Stephen. *Promises to Keep: How Leaders and the Public Respond to Saving and Retirement.* A Report from the Public Agenda in collaboration with Employee Benefit Research Institute, Public Agenda. Washington D.C. 1994.

Feldstein, Martin. "Social Security, Induced Retirement, and Aggregate Capital Accumulation." *Journal of Political Economy* Vol. 5, no. 82, 1974.

Feldstein, Martin. "International Differences in Social Security and Saving." *Journal of Public Economics* Vol. 14, 1980.

Feldstein, Martin. "Social Security and Savings: New Time Series Evidence." NBER Working Paper No. 5054. Cambridge, Mass., National Bureau of Economic Research, 1995.

Feldstein, Martin. "The Missing Piece in Policy Analysis: Social Security Reform." NBER Working Paper No. 5413. Cambridge, Mass., National Bureau of Economic Research, 1996.

Folbre, Nancy. *Who Pays For The Kids: Gender and the Structures of Constraints* London, Routledge, 1994.

Ghilarducci, Teresa. *Labor's Capital: the Economics and Politics of Private Pensions*. Cambridge, Ma., MIT Press, 1992.

Kingson, Eric R. and James H. Schultz, editors. *Social Security in the 21ˢᵗ Century*. New York, Oxford University Press, 1997

Munnell, Alicia. "The Impact of Social Security on Private Saving", *National Tax Journal*, Vol. 27, No. 4, pp 553-67, 1974.

Olson, Laura Katz. *The Political Economy of Ageing : The State, Private Power, and Social Welfare*. New York : Columbia University Press, 1982.

Pampel, Fred and John Williamson. *Old Age Security in Comparative Perspective*, New York, Oxford University Press, 1993

Pierson, Paul. "The Politics of Pension Reform." in Banting and Boadway, editors. 273-294, 1996..

Quadagno, Jill and John Myles. "Recent Trends in Public Pension Reform: A Comparative View" in Banting and Boadway, editors. 247 – 273, 1996.

Reno, Virginia P. "The Role of Pensions in Retirement Income," *Pensions in a Changing Economy.* Employee Benefits Research Institute. Washington D.C., 1993.

Sandell, Steven.   "Women and Social Security," presentation to the Advisory Council on Social Security, October 24, 1994.

Schnarch, David. *Passionate Marriage* New York, W.W. Norton, 1996.

Schieber, Sylvester J, and John B. Shoven. "The Consequences of Population Ageing on Private Pension Fund, Saving and Asset Markets" Prepared for the NBER-JCER joint conference, The Economics of Ageing, September 14-16, at Hakone, Japan, NBER Working paper series no. 4665. Cambridge, Ma, National Bureau of Economic Research, 1994.

Steurele, Eugene and Jon, Bakija *Retooling Social Security for the 20th Century.* Washington D.C., The Urban Institute, 1995.

Singletary, Michelle and Albert B. Crenshaw. "When Credit is Due" *Washington Post Weekly* Edition, December 2-8, 1996.

Tritch, Teresa. "The Privatization of Social Security: Who Wins and Who Loses?" *Money* April 1996, 119 - 122.

U.S. HEW. *Report of the HEW Task Force on the Treatment of Women under Social Security,* February, 1978.

Wolfson, , Michael and Brian Murphy. "Ageing and Canada's Public Sector" in Banting and Boadway, editors. 69 – 98, 1996.

World Bank Report, (primary author Estelle James) *Averting the Old Age Crises.* New York, Oxford University Press, 1994.

14   A NEW SOCIAL SECURITY: TRADITIONAL SOCIAL SECURITY PLUS A PENSION SUPPLEMENT[1]

Yung-Ping Chen

Introduction

Almost everywhere, in industrialized and developing nations alike, the same demanding question keeps surfacing: How can we provide for our older population, public or private approaches? Existing public programs in most parts of the world are being scrutinized. There is no denying that the costs of social security programs have been on the rise, and if the trend is allowed to persist, might climb to financially unsustainable levels. In response, dismantling social security has been suggested, and strong advocacy exists for private systems of individual savings and investments. But in reality, like public programs, private systems come with their own potentially troubling downside. Endorsing a mix of public and private approaches, I propose a plan that can combine the best of both: the financial guarantees that only a public social security system can provide, coupled with an opportunity to achieve the higher investment returns offered in the private market.

In this paper I describe and critique the three reform plans offered by the 1994-96 U.S. Advisory Council on Social Security (1997). I conclude that all three plans suffer from many limitations which outweigh their respective major advantages. Then, incorporating many salubrious features of each of these plans while avoiding many of their more serious disadvantages, I present my plan to combine the traditional defined-benefit social insurance account with a new defined-contribution individual pension supplement, thus creating what I call a "New Social Security," in order to implement public and private approaches.

One Council, Three Plans

In the United States, the 1994-96 Advisory Council on Social Security was unable to reach consensus on how to restore long-range solvency to the program while also improving rates of return for future beneficiaries. In the end, rival plans were proposed by three factions among the 13-member Council. Each has merit, although all entail major problems.

The Maintain Benefits (MB) plan, voted by six members, offered one important advantage: it preserves Social Security essentially as is, thus continuing the program based on social insurance principles. To raise the rates of return, this plan recommends only an investigation into the advisability of investing trust fund money in stocks as a means of generating more revenue for the Social Security program. Without the higher returns projected from investments in equities, however, one-third of Social Security's long-range deficit will persist.

The Personal Security Account (PSA) plan, voted by five members, would comprise a two-tier system as a replacement for Social Security. The first tier would provide a flat-rate benefit. The second-tier's benefit would emanate from a mandatory "personal security account," to be managed by the individual account owner. This saving/investment account would be funded from 5 percentage points of the 6.2 percent payroll tax currently paid by the employee. The expectation under this plan is that higher yields from investments in private financial markets would improve the overall rates of return. The idea of investing one's own money, in the hope of greater gains, may appeal to some workers, but private investments are all subject to market risks and further, this plan requires additional payroll taxes, as well as borrowing by the federal Government (with requisite repayment), to pay for the lengthy transition (some 70 years) from the present program to this new one.

The Individual Account (IA) plan, voted by two members, would reduce benefits under the existing Social Security program to fit within the current payroll tax rate of 12.4% and would add on a mandatory saving/investment account, called "individual account," which the individual account owner allocates among a choice of Government-administered funds. Unlike the PSA plan, which would fund its saving/investment accounts by redirecting part of the employees payroll taxes, the saving/investment account under the IA plan would be funded by *additional* contributions from employees. Like the PSA plan, the expectation with this plan is improved rates of return, derived from the higher earnings that would accrue to these accounts. While some people might welcome this sort of add-on, it is uncertain whether lower-paid employees could afford to or would willingly contribute more than they do now under the payroll taxation.

Individual Accounts Not the Same as Pensions

These plans reflect three very different visions about the best way to provide retirement income in the future. The MB plan emphasizes the central importance of collective assistance under social insurance, while the PSA and IA plans rely, instead, more on saving and investment efforts by individuals privately (thus commonly known as privatization). But none of these plans would change the present U. S. retirement income policy in a way that would achieve a better balance between Social Security and private pensions. Currently, in fact, only about one-third of individuals age 65 and older have pension income, and, for most of them, income from this source is not very significant. Looking toward the future, we can anticipate similar problems, because only about one-half of the present work force are covered by private pensions. And the pension benefits for many of the people who do receive them will be meager indeed.

While the individualized accounts proposed under the PSA and IA plans are designed to increase retirement income, they are savings accounts and not the same as private pensions because these accounts are funded entirely by employees.

Unless private pension coverage is universalized in a way that will be accessible and affordable to everyone, pressure on Social Security to raise benefits could intensify – further threatening the financial health of the program. Mandating private pensions is one possible solution, but it is quite likely that many low-wage workers and small businesses just could not afford, or would not be willing, to pay the additional contributions required. It may be argued that both PSA and IA plans are designed to universalize private pension coverage by means of their individualized saving/investment accounts. However, mandating such accounts brings the same problem with affordability or willpower.

Is there, then, a way by which the best features of the three plans could be utilized in a plan that would not be plagued by their drawbacks? That is, can we preserve Social Security essentially as we know it, as in the MB plan, without leaving (as MB does) one-third of the long-range deficit still to be addressed? Can we create private investment accounts by redirecting a portion of the current payroll tax, as in the PSA plan, without the new burden of additional taxes and Government borrowing needed to finance the transition? Can we add private investment accounts to Social Security, as in the IA plan, without imposing new payroll taxes or additional contributions from employees? In other words, can we eliminate the long-range deficit and possibly also improve the rate of return for future beneficiaries by a plan that adopts the best features in the three plans while steering clear of their major disadvantages?

A New Social Security (The SS-PS Plan)

Happily, there is a way: supplement Social Security with private pensions, by dividing the current Social Security program into two components, a defined benefit social insurance account and a defined contribution supplementary pension account. We can do this, and still keep the *combined* costs for both accounts at the current payroll tax rate – 12.4% – for the next 24 years. The defined benefit account is the traditional Social Security program, while the defined contribution account would function as a *supplementary* pension program. In other words, Social Security remains as a defined benefit plan; the supplementary pension would be a defined contribution plan. Under this plan, then, the Social Security program would operate on a pay-as-you-go (PAYGO) method of financing. The pension supplement program would be financed with the 1.6 percentage points of the current 12.4 percent FICA rate that are not needed to pay benefits.

I call this plan "New Social Security" or the "Social Security plus Pension Supplement (SS-PS) plan."

Under this new plan, a new mandatory pension account (with immediate vesting) for *all* employees – those who don't have pension coverage now, as well as those who do – will be established; all employees covered under Social Security would gain a slice of fully vested pension protection that they could take from one job to another, irrespective of the length of service in each. Too many of today's theoretically "covered" employees will in fact never receive employer-sponsored pension benefits, because they do not stay at the job long enough to meet their employer's vesting requirements.

One question quickly comes to mind: When the FICA rate for Social Security returns to 12.4%, in 2023, how would the mandatory pension supplement be funded? Then, I propose that we no longer require these accounts. Workers would continue to save voluntarily, I believe, if favorable experiences accrue to those accounts. It is also possible that if experience has been good and the pension supplement account is "large", a person might choose to stop future contributions. On the other hand, if experiences are unfavorable, then why mandate? Should the experiences turn out mixed, as is likely, a sensible policy would be to allow individual choice of saving or not saving. In fact, the next policy challenge in some countries which mandate personal accounts is how to transform them into voluntary ones. That transformation is part of the SS-PS plan. Implementing voluntary accounts now appears ineffective. Making such accounts mandatory in the future seems unwarranted.

One objection to SS-PS may be that it would be very expensive and inefficient to maintain many small accounts. For example, a 1.6 percent contribution rate will only yield $320 a year for a $20,000 earner. This problem would be serious if these accounts were individually held and managed. However, these accounts could be held and managed by a central authority with a limited number of investment options ranging from all bonds to all equities and somewhere in between for the account holders to choose from on a periodic basis. Like the IA plan, pension supplement accounts under SS-PS would be paid out as an annuity.

Private Accounts as an Experiment

To avoid the morass of endless debate or precipitated adoption of legislation based only on hypothetical projections, I propose a national demonstration project. Let us set up the proposed defined contribution pension account for every Social Security participant for a period of 10 to 15 years during the next two decades, during which the FICA rate will remain at its current level. There is an important recent precedent for this type of experimentation: the pilot study on medical savings accounts included as one provision in the Health Insurance Portability and Accountability Act of 1996 (the Kassebaum-Kennedy bill).

From the data we collect about these private accounts, we will learn, among other things, about the investment behavior of people by key demographic and economic variables (age, sex, wage/salary, etc.). For example, we can find out whether women in general are more risk-adverse than men, and whether low earners are less sophisticated investors. We can learn some particulars about investment performance – who makes out well versus at the other extreme who loses inordinately. And we can study patterns of borrowing from these accounts, finding out the reasons why people take out loans for purposes other than retirement and how likely they are to repay these loans on time.

The proposed demonstration project raises a significant question about the safety of retirement income, one of the major concerns about privatization: What if a worker were to lose much or even everything he or she has put into the supplementary pension account during the demonstration period? *This possible scenario highlights how the SS component of SS-PS proves its worth.* By design, the SS portion of SS-PS provides a floor of income protection supported by the PAYGO rates proposed. Any benefit that accrues from the PS portion is an add-on. So, even in the extreme case when the PS yields nothing, all they would lose is the add-on and they still will be guaranteed their Social Security benefits.

Absent a demonstration project that is mandated by law as suggested, we will never be able to move beyond polemics and speculation. Because the enabling legislation will include a sunset provision, the proposed time-limited demonstration will not commit the country to a permanent policy shift, thus extricating us from a potentially lengthy impasse.

When further changes become necessary in future years, the process will doubtless generate new policy conflicts. But the debate will be on firmer ground, because the demonstration will have yielded important "laboratory" data of a sort that is usually unavailable to social scientists. Because of the changes in the macroeconomic environment and new trends in financial behavior of individuals and households, these empirical data may only serve as a relatively rough guide to the future. However, information from the demonstration project will be far more valuable than any data we could obtain by other means. In addition, the SS-PS demonstration project will convey another benefit: flexibility in policy formulation, based on hard data rather than hypothetical speculation. To prevent the demonstration from becoming an obstacle to balancing the budget or to the Treasury's borrowing from the Social Security trust funds, the year when the unified federal budget is in balance should be selected as the starting date.

Conclusion

In short, the SS-PS plan would achieve the two critical objectives spelled out by the Advisory Council – restoring solvency to Social Security and making it possible for future beneficiaries to achieve higher rates of return – without the troubling disadvantages inevitably associated with the three plans it has suggested. Even more important, SS-PS is designed to strike a better balance between Social Security and private pensions, a vital goal in our developing national retirement income policy that is not addressed by any of the Council's three plans.

Notes

1. This plan was first presented in "Bolster Private Pensions while Saving Social Security," in *Contingencies*, American Academy of Actuaries, July-August, 1997, pp.40-43.

References

United States, 1997. 1994-96 Advisory Council on Social Security, Report, Volume 1, Findings and Recommendations. Washington: DC:. U.S. Government Printing Office.

Index